Medicine Man
to Missionary

Medicine Man to Missionary

Missionaries as Agents of Change among
the Indians of Southern Ontario, 1784-1867

Elizabeth Graham

Peter Martin Associates Limited

The book has been published with the help of a grant from the Social Science Research Council of Canada, using funds provided by the Canada Council.

Design: Diana McElroy

Canadian Shared Cataloguing in Publication Data

Graham, Elizabeth
    Medicine man to missionary : missionaries as agents of change among the Indians of Southern Ontario, 1784-1867 / by Elizabeth Graham.—

                (Canadian experience series)

1. Indians of North America — Ontario — Missions. 2. Indians of North America — Ontario — Social life and customs. 3. Ontario — History — To 1867.   I. Title.

E78.05G7   970.413
ISBN: 0-88778-077-6; 0-88778-078-4 (pbk.)

Peter Martin Associates Limited
35 Britain Street, Toronto, Canada M5A 1R7

United Kingdom: Books Canada, 1 Bedford Road, London N2
United States: Books Canada, 33 East Tupper St., Buffalo, N.Y. 14203

Acknowledgements

This book is part of a thesis prepared at the University of Toronto. Research for the thesis was financed by the Canada Council, the Province of Ontario Graduate Fellowship, and my husband. I should like to thank the Archivists and Librarians at: The United Church Archives; Church House; the Department of Public Records and Archives of Ontario; the University of Toronto Library; Trinity, Knox, and Emmanual College Libraries; the Toronto Public Library; Regis College Library in Toronto; the Public Archives of Canada, Ottawa; the United Society for the Propagation of the Gospel in Foreign Parts; the Church Missionary Society; the Guildhall Library; and Moravian House, in London; the Moravian Archives in Bethlehem, Pa.; and the Canadian Baptist Historical Collection at McMaster Divinity College, Hamilton.

CONTENTS

INTRODUCTION TO THE
CANADIAN EXPERIENCE SERIES

Each of the monographs in this Series deals with a particular aspect of Canadian society and is based on professional research in one of the social sciences. The editors and publishers of Canadian Experience designed the Series to meet two particular needs. One is the need for inexpensive and readable accounts of life in Canada, produced under entirely Canadian auspices but available to readers outside Canada as well as in this country. The other is the need for clear and unpretentious statements of the assumptions and processes underlying professional social research—information which is essential to beginning students of the social sciences and of increasing relevence to the general reader.

Two features of the Series may be noted in this respect. First, each of the books will include, as this one does, an explicit and unusually detailed statement of research methods and methodology. This appears in every case as a separate section or chapter, so that the body of the work which follows, although necessarily structured by the author's approach, may be left free of unexplained concepts and professional jargon, and so that students may see clearly that a method of research can be described or assessed only in relation to the context of research and the problem with which it is concerned. Teachers of social science at all levels know that accounts of what social scientists do are meaningless unless all three facets—method, context and problem—are related and presented together.

Second, the work behind the titles in Canadian Experience is not the product of one single professional discipline. Recent trends indicate that the boundaries between the various social sciences are becoming less rigid and less useful. No scientific discipline can now afford to restrict itself to a single theoretical framework: approaches vary within single institutions and cross and re-cross the boundaries of university departments. While a variety of approaches to social research are presented in this Series, the variation does not necessarily tally with professional labels—although the professional calibre of each writer is established and his or her affiliation specified where it is relevent. We would hope and expect that each volume will be of interest along a gamut of social scientific persuasions as well as outside academic circles.

This Series is both more eclectic and methodologically more specific than has been usual at this level. Its focus on studies of Canada could be justified simply on the grounds that many Canadians are now demanding new dimensions to their national identity: they want to know what it means to be a Canadian. But we are also convinced that the vitality and variety of the "Canadian experience" has been consistently underestimated, and that these monographs on Canadian society and research offer insights into situations and social processes which are significant to us all.

—Sandra Wallman
General Editor

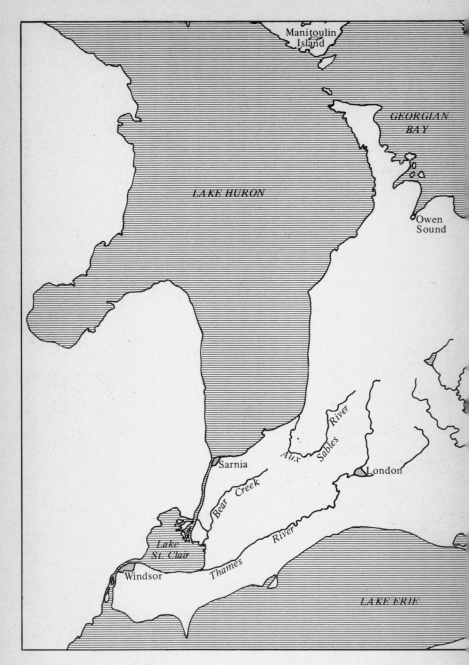

GEORGIAN
BAY

Penetanguishene

Balsam
Lake

Lake
Simcoe

Holland Landing

Lake
Scugog

Peterborough

Rice Lake

Belleville

Bay of Quinte

Cobourg

Credit

River

Toronto

LAKE ONTARIO

Hamilton

Grand

River

LAKE ERIE

CHAPTER I

INTRODUCTION

The aim of this book is to study the roles of missionaries in the development of the Indian reserve communities of southern Ontario. In the nineteenth century the goal of Christian missionaries to the "heathen" was not only to teach them about Christianity, but to "civilize" them, or teach them the technology, customs and niceties of European society.* With this dual goal, missionaries acted not only as ministers of religion, but tried to assume authority in those spheres of cultural and social life into which they could introduce civilization: subsistence and technology, politics and government, education and morality, and health. Missionaries, therefore, played direct roles as ministers of religion, farmers and artisans, politicians and administrators, schoolteachers, doctors and social workers, and were important agents of social change.

During the period, 1784 to 1867, which is being considered in this book, there were considerable changes in the social structure and culture of the Indians of southern Ontario. These changes were most noticeable among the Ojibwa, who changed from autonomous bands of hunting and gathering peoples to settled reserve communities of peasant farmers; but were also important for the Iroquois and Delaware groups. Coinciding with these changes was the work of missionaries who took up residence with the Indians and participated in the affairs of the communities in order to accomplish their goal of civilization and Christianization. The theme of this book is to examine the kinds of changes they brought about and the success† they achieved as innovators.

Methods and Sources

This book relies entirely on historical documents, thereby differing from the usual approach to social anthropology in which analysis is based on

---

*Civilization was equated by the missionaries with European culture and for convenience this is the sense in which the term is used in the book.

†The terms "success" and "progress" refer throughout the book to the missionaries' goals.

evidence gathered by participant observation during fieldwork. However, processes of social change are of primary concern to anthropologists and the concepts used to interpret the data are those developed by social anthropologists. It would not be inappropriate to call this study a social history of particular groups at a particular time.

Ventures into social history by social anthropologists have at least two aims. One is to try to go beyond the approach to social change studies as a chronicle and measurement of culture trait changes, in an attempt to understand the processes of social change. What makes people welcome, or resist, changes? Do primitive peoples in fact have any choice of action when they come in contact with western society? The other aim is to expand the traditional field of social anthropology and add the dimension of time. Formerly, social anthropologists studied the social relationships of a community as if they occurred at one point in time. However, all social relationships occur in time, as well as in space, and in order to gain a more balanced perspective, social relationships should be studied as they occur in time and space.

There is no attempt to examine the traditional culture and then measure acculturation. There is a dearth of material from which to reconstruct the cultures of the various groups, and extrapolation of culture from other groups described at different times in different places would probably be invalid because of the unique historical conditions relevant to the groups being studied here. All of the groups (except the Wyandots) were immigrant to the area after the sixteenth century and had been in contact with whites for as many years. Since changes resulting from geographical adjustment and contact with whites must have been considerable, and had been occurring for a long time before the missionaries arrived, it would not be possible to describe the "traditional" culture.

Similarly, although the study is ethnohistorical inasmuch as historical documents are used and some attempt is made to reconstruct events and social processes, the method of "upstreaming" (working back from the present) is not used because of the big time gap between 1867 and 1974. There may be a difference of emphasis on the kinds of documents usually considered valid by ethnohistorians. In this study the analysis of social relationships and changes resulting from these relationships is important, and documents containing no factual material but attitudes, opinions and speculation, are also of value in reconstructing the content of relationships.

The main problem in this kind of study, and one that has deterred many anthropologists from making the attempt, is the difficulty of obtaining information. If the anthropologist is trying to find out why people do what they do, one way to find out is to ask them. To assess whether the answer is the one the person thinks the anthropologist would like to hear, the one he should give, what he believes to be true, or whether there are circumstances of which the person is unaware but which affect his behaviour, the anthropologist should also question the person's friends, neighbours and enemies, and find out as many of the relevant circumstances as possible. These aspects of a situation are probably difficult to discover in a face-to-face situation, and may be impossible in a historical study. One side of the story may be recorded, but not the others. I have attempted to fill in as many of the gaps as possible by using not only missionary reports and writings, but also government reports, and petitions and letters from Indians. There is, unfortunately, a built-in bias in material written by Indians because there were no written accounts before literacy, and literacy and conversion to a particular religious denomination usually went together.

As this is a study of missionary influence, I have relied mainly on missionary reports, and missionaries' diaries, letters, and books. Nineteenth century missionaries believed unquestioningly in the superiority of western society and civilization. They judged Indian culture in terms of their own values and had no idea of looking at, or accepting, Indian culture in terms of Indian values. As a result they were generally not interested in describing or even discovering Indian customs and beliefs, except insofar as these impeded Christianization and civilization. The mission reports vary tremendously in their contents and usefulness. The Methodists wrote annual reports which date back to the beginning of the missions and continue to the present. These have full information on the number of converts, members of the church, deaths, baptisms, etc., each year, but they have to be supplemented by more descriptive accounts of the mission work found in other newspapers and journals, and in the personal accounts by missionaries. The Church of England reports vary in their detail. The Society for the Propagation of the Gospel has skeleton annual reports. The reports of the New England Company are quite detailed, but are concerned with the progress of education and farming operations, rather than the personalities of the people in the congregation, and reports are not available for all years. At Moraviantown the missionaries left a very detailed record of the mission work, with life histories of the members, particularly in the early years of the mission. The Roman

Catholic reports are more concerned with the opposition they met than the progress of the mission, and the Baptist reports contain very little information. Government reports provide some useful descriptive and statistical information on all the communities, particularly the reports of 1847 and 1858. The Record Group 10 collection in the Public Archives of Canada is the only good source of material written directly by Indians. It is in the form of petitions and letters of complaint to the Governor-General and other officials.

There are many gaps in the records, and information for most of the communities is very incomplete. Another problem is that some of the material contains much of a factual nature, but not nearly enough opinion or description for interpretation of the facts; while other material is entirely based on opinion, with no data to back it up, and consists of complaints of one group or individual about another group or individual, and the interpretation of people's actions and motives rather than a chronological account of events. It is the task of the anthropologist to interpret and put together the material as best he can; he must sort out the various biases and their significance, also recognizing his own bias while attempting to remain as impartial as possible in the application of sociological concepts.

The first step in ordering the mass of data collected was to arrange events in a chronological and spatial order to show how and where the missionaries went about their work, and to decide on suitable chronological and spatial boundaries. The year 1784 was chosen to begin the period, as the year the first Christian Indians (Mohawks) arrived in the area. Between 1784 and 1822 there was very little proselytization, but after 1822 Methodist missionaries attempted large scale proselytization in southern Ontario. Chapter two describes the state of the missions between 1784 and 1830. In 1830 the Government began to participate in schemes to civilize the Indians and thus changed the character of Indian-white relations. There was considerable competition between missionaries and government agents at this time. Towards the end of the period there was a waning of enthusiasm for the work of civilizing and Christianizing the Indians. This shows up in the lack of information about the communities, and makes it difficult to find a cut-off point for the study; 1867 is an arbitrary choice. Chapter three contains a discussion of government and missionary society policies and a review of events in the communities.

Spatially it was equally difficult to find cut-off points, because of historical, geographical and ethnic variables. The geographical area chosen (southern Ontario) included many different ethnic groups (Huron, Iroquois, Delaware, Ojibwa, etc.) and was geographically and socially heterogeneous. Originally Manitoulin Island was included in the area as it was historically significant in the government scheme of 1830. However, Manitoulin Island could not be included without considering communities on Georgian Bay and Lake Superior which had different geographical and historical conditions, and it seemed more practical to exclude them all. Similarly, although the Mohawk reserve at Cornwall (St. Regis) is in southern Ontario, it was excluded because it has more historical ties with reserves in Quebec.

The next step was to look at topics and to analyze the work of the missionaries according to the various roles that they played. The term "role" has been defined in many ways, and used in many ways. Banton (1965:29) has described a role as "a set of norms and expectations applied to the incumbent of a particular position", but the role of missionary is such a general one that it contains many differing roles in itself (cf. Wallman, 1974) — particular facets being defined by the context or situation in which the role is played (see Nadel, 1957).

The various roles played by the missionaries in the Indian communities are important in regarding the missionaries not only as a source of change, but also as an integral part of the social structure of changing Indian society. These roles include their spheres of influence in changing the belief systems and religious organization; their effects on the social organization based on their conception of Christian morality; and the roles they played in secular spheres such as education, politics, economics, technology and medicine. Questions to be examined are the ways in which the missionaries interpreted or performed their roles, how many roles they played, and whether all or some of these roles are necessarily contained in the role of missionary. These roles are described in chapters four, five and six.

During the course of research and analysis, it became apparent that the power struggle between Indians, government agents, and missionaries, for the right to make decisions about the affairs of the Indians, was crucial to understanding the effectiveness of the missionary role and the attitudes of the Indians to conversion and change. The view of missionaries, not only as innovators but as part of the whole political system, leads to the analysis of the data in terms of political power relations and the changing patterns of power relationships over time (see Graham 1973).

Such an analysis is, unfortunately, beyond the scope of this book, but some discussion of government policies is included because it is impossible to divorce missionary work from government policy. This book attempts an analysis of missionaries in terms of their roles as agents of change with a combination of synchronic and diachronic approaches. The very fact that, for the sake of clarity, these are separated in the format of the book, indicates that no satisfactory way has been found to analyze relationships in time, and relationships in space, congruently. However, in the concluding chapter, an attempt will be made to sum up and assess the significant patterns of change that emerge.

The Indians

The history of the Indian settlement of southern Ontario is a record of considerable migration and upheaval. Prior to the seventeenth century, the area was occupied by several related Iroquoian groups (Huron, Petun, Neutral). The story of the Jesuit missions to the Hurons from 1602 to 1650 is a well-known one. However, disease and raids from the Iroquois during the seventeenth century finally resulted in the disappearance and dispersal of most of the Huron groups. In the following decades Ojibwa Indians from the north moved into the area, clashing with the Iroquois, but eventually established themselves over the whole region. By 1784 there were several Indian groups living in southern Ontario. Various Ojibwa groups were the most numerous and widespread. There were Iroquois of the Six Nations on the Grand River and Mohawks at the Bay of Quinte; there were Munsee Delawares on the Thames River, followed by Moravian Delawares in 1792; there was a small group of Hurons at Amherstburg.

a) *The Ojibwa*

The Ojibwa, or Chippewa as they were called in the early literature, lived between the northern shores of Lakes Huron and Superior, and the edge of the prairies, before contact with Europeans. In historic times these Ojibwa expanded northwestward with the fur trade, and southeastward into southern Ontario after the rout of the Hurons by the Iroquois in the seventeenth century (Jenness 1955:277).

The Ojibwa Indians were divided into numerous bands that possessed their own hunting territories and were politically independent of each other. By 1784 southern Ontario was inhabited by many Ojibwa bands:

the Mississauga Indians lived in the area bordering on Lake Ontario, while there were Ojibwa groups in southwestern Ontario and on the shores of Lake Huron, and to the north around Lake Simcoe and Georgian Bay. All these bands relied on hunting and gathering for their subsistence.

At the close of the American revolution, when the British were restricted to Canada, the land of southern Ontario, then part of the western province of Quebec, became very valuable to them. As settlement grew, the Ojibwa were persuaded to sell their land to the Crown. By 1822, the Ojibwa had sold most of the southern part of the area, reserving small tracts of land on the St. Clair River and the Credit River. However, the bands were still able to live much as they had formerly, by hunting and gathering.

b) *The Six Nations Indians*

The Six Nations Indians who came to Canada were members of the Confederacy, or League, of nations composed of Mohawks, Onondagas, Cayugas, Senecas, Oneidas and Tuscaroras. The Six Nations Indians had supported the British during the war, and when their lands were forfeited to the Americans, they were promised land by the British. They were originally settled on land in the Cataraqui district of the Bay of Quinte, but Joseph Brant, a Mohawk leader, negotiated for the land of the Grand River valley. In 1784, they were granted land six miles deep on either side of the Grand River from its source to its mouth. When the site was actually surveyed by the British, the headwaters of the river were not included. This fact and the proclamation itself have been an unending source of controversy, since Brant interpreted the proclamation as tantamount to full national recognition of the Mohawk nation, an inference which was later strongly denied by the British. Brant's policy during the first few years of settlement was to sell and lease lands to white settlers, and by 1798, 350,000 acres of the original 570,000 acre grant had been transferred (Johnston 1964:xxxi-liv). The Indians who had originally moved to the Grand River consisted of 450 Mohawks, 380 Cayugas, 200 Onondagas, 125 Tuscaroras, 75 Senecas, and a few Oneidas, Delawares, Tutelos and Nanticokes. Some of the Mohawks remained at the Bay of Quinte.

c) *The Moravian Indians*

The Moravian Indians came to Canada with their missionaries, David

Zeisberger and Gottlob Sensemann, in 1792. They consisted of 151 Delaware Indians who had become Christians and were refugees from the wars in the United States. They settled on the Thames River, and in 1793 it was established that the Moravians could have land six miles deep, fronting the river on both sides (Bliss 1885:320). In 1803 the Governor of Canada gave orders that the 25,000 acres allotted by the Government for the use of the Christian Indians should be measured and secured to them (PA, vol. III:260). In 1813 the settlement was completely destroyed by the American army, and the Indians were forced to flee. When the trouble died down and the Indians returned to Fairfield in 1816, it was decided that the new village would be built a little higher up the river on the opposite bank (PA, vol. VI:253).

d) *The Munsees*

The Munsees were also Delaware Indians who settled on the Thames River at the close of the American revolutionary war. They were squatters on Ojibwa land, and relationships between the Ojibwa and the Munsees were strained.

e) *Wyandot*

In 1791 a reserve was confirmed to a number of Wyandot, or Huron Indians, near Amherstburg — a part of their ancient possessions.

The Missionaries

During the eighteenth century in England and Europe, many missionary societies were formed to accompany the spread of colonization in different parts of the world. Early in the eighteenth century the Moravian Missionary Society, with its North American headquarters in Bethlehem, Pennsylvania, and the Church of England Society for the Propagation of the Gospel in Foreign Parts (SPG), sent missionaries to the North American Indians. The Moravian missionaries worked with the Delaware Indians, and the SPG missionaries worked with the Mohawks. When the Mohawks and the "Moravian Indians" moved to Canada towards the end of the century, they maintained their connections with the churches. In the nineteenth century, with the general settlement of Upper Canada, several other missionary societies sent missionaries to the Indians, and they acquired land or attached themselves to Indian groups. In the 1820's, the Methodist Episcopal Church Missionary Society sent missionaries from the

United States, and the New England Company of London, England (primarily Church of England) started a mission. In the 1830's, the Wesleyan Methodist Missionary Society sent missionaries from England, and in the 1840's, the Society of Jesus sent Jesuits from Quebec to Walpole Island, and the New York State Baptist Missionary Society started a mission at Tuscarora. Later arrivals were the Church of England Church Missionary Society (CMS) and the Congregationalists.

CHAPTER II

EARLY MISSIONS AND THE
CONVERSION OF THE MISSISSAUGAS

The period between 1784, when the British began to get involved with Indians in the region that later became Upper Canada, and 1830, when the Government decided to launch a scheme for the civilization of the Indians, was largely one of internal autonomy for Indian communities. However, during this period the Indians lost most of their land and experienced the beginnings of the missionary movement, and both these factors were significant in the loss of that autonomy. This chapter is concerned with describing the missionary movement. First, however, the policy of the Indian Department is described, showing that interaction between Indians and the Government was confined to land settlements, annuity payments and the distribution of presents. Following this is an account of the Moravian mission at New Fairfield and the unsuccessful attempt to convert some Ojibwa, and the Church of England association with Mohawks at Tyendinaga and the Six Nations with the establishment of resident missionaries at the Six Nations reserve in the latter part of the period. The bulk of the chapter is devoted to a description of Methodist missions and the overwhelming impact of Christianity on the Mississauga Indians. This was the most successful period of missionary endeavour.

The Indian Department

In the early days the administration of the Indian Department was in the hands of the military. In 1782, Sir John Johnson was appointed Superintendent General, and continued in this office until 1828, but his continued absence from the country made it necessary to create the office of Deputy Superintendent General in 1794. In 1828 a General Order in Council abolished the position of Superintendent General and created in its place the office of Chief Superintendent of Indian Affairs, an appointment which was held by Major-General H. C. Darling until 1830 (RG10, inventory:1).

Before the turn of the century the main duty of the Indian Department was to keep the Indians loyal to the Crown, and much depended on the personal influence and power of the officials in the Department, and the issue of presents to the Indians which started after the Revolutionary war. With the settlement of Upper Canada, the officials of the Indian Department, and particularly the agents of Sir John Johnson, were busy negotiating land purchases and treaties with the Indians. The British considered that the Indians had title to the land, and negotiated purchases or treaties for its surrender. Between 1781 and 1830 the Indians surrendered large areas of southern Ontario to the Government.

The Missionaries

Moravians

The only group to have permanent contact with missionaries before 1822 were the Moravian Indians, who constituted a community by virtue of their connection with the Moravian missionaries. Membership in the community depended on being Christian and agreeing to live by the rules of the community. David Zeisberger, the missionary who brought the Indians to Canada, made the following entry in his diary for June 2, 1793:

> In the afternoon our statutes and church-ordinances were made known to all the inhabitants, and the brethren were admonished to obey them, so that they might not only have the name of Christian Indians, but might show it by their behaviour. If, however, these ordinances did not please them, or were too severe, the door was always open for them to go, yes, he who had no mind so to live would do better to go and not to plague himself in vain, for the land was given to the Christian Indians alone to live on, and not to the savages. (Bliss 1885:314)

There were always two or three missionaries and their wives living with the Indians, and when the congregation was forced to go into exile during the war of 1812, one brother, Denke, stayed with the Indians until they could return to Fairfield.

The close connection between the Fairfield community and the Munceytown a few miles up the river, brought several contacts between the missionaries and the Munsees, although these were not always of a strictly religious character. There was much intermarriage and visiting between the communities, and several individuals came from Munceytown to live at Fairfield, or to be converted. Zeisberger commented that the Munsees:

> . . . although they have no disposition to be converted, yet can

not keep away from us. Now and then they have to come to
see us, and then they always hear the word of life, and when
they are dying, something which they have heard among us oc-
curs to them, and they long to come to us, when usually they
can no longer attain thereto. (Bliss 1885:470)

A significant conversion took place in 1816 on the deathbed of Onim, a
preacher among the Indians:

. . . he used to dissuade them by all the means in his power of
embracing the doctrines of the whites. For, said he, their skin is
white, and our skin is brown, and our whole manner of life is
entirely different from theirs. Of course they must also have a
different way to happiness and those Indians who embrace their
doctrine are altogether deceived. He taught the existence of
three gods, a brown, a white and a black god, and that each nation
ought to live conformably to the directions received from the God
of their colour . . .   (PA, vol. VI:301)

According to Onim, it was a remark made to him by one of the Christian
women that made him worried about his spiritual state, and when he was
taken sick on his way to Munceytown, he sent for the Indian assistant
who spoke to him. He was converted, and then baptized. There was no
attempt made by the missionaries to proselytize the Munsee Indians as a
group, nor was there any attempt by the Munsee band to get a missionary.

Similarly, there was no attempt by the frequent Ojibwa visitors to
Fairfield to get a missionary, though they often attended church meetings on their visits. In 1801, Brother Denke attempted to start a mission
among the Ojibwa of the St. Clair River and Walpole Island region. Denke
took three Delawares and travelled to the St. Clair River where he met a
group of thirty Ojibwa. Most of the men were away hunting, including
the head chief, Nangi, and the subchief. Denke told them his purpose,
and the Indians replied that they would be willing to have a teacher, but
they would have to consult Nangi. The Delaware with him described
their conversion and the improvement in their condition since they had
had a teacher, and the Chippewas promised to renounce their "heathen
dances and ceremonies and intemperate habits" and ask Nangi for land
for a mission house. Later Denke met Nangi and eight head men of the
Chippewa and Ottawa bands and was granted a plot of ground. In 1802,
he returned to start the mission, but soon afterwards an accident forced
him to return to Fairfield, and during his absence local white people persuaded the Indians that the acceptance of a missionary had caused sickness among them. Nangi pointed out that the white people had as much

sickness, and when Denke returned, Nangi was friendly with him. But the Indians thought Nangi was responsible for the prohibition on the sale of liquor to Indians, by the American Government, and were not pleased with him. Denke left the mission soon after this, and the mission was abandoned (Jacobson 1806:141-51).

After the war of 1812, the Fairfield community was rebuilt on the other side of the river, and renamed New Fairfield. In 1822 the community received an increase in numbers with the arrival of some other Moravian Indians from the United States. At the beginning of 1822, there were 160 people at New Fairfield. At the end of 1829, there were 202 people. The diaries during this decade were much concerned with domestic matters, and with the state of the church and its members.

The Church of England

Before the American Revolution, when the Mohawks were at Fort Hunter, they had been sent missionaries by the Society for the Propagation of the Gospel in Foreign Parts (SPG), but when they moved to Canada they did not have resident missionaries. In June of 1784, the Rev. John Stuart, who had been a missionary with the Mohawks at Fort Hunter from 1770 to 1781, visited the Mohawks at their settlement near Niagara and officiated in their Church, baptizing seventy-eight infants and five adults. There was an Indian clerk who read prayers on Sundays, and Stuart remarked that he was very pleased with the devotion of the people. When the Mohawks moved to the Grand River, the British Government built a church for them, and they were visited after 1793 by the clergyman for the Niagara region.

The SPG sent their first resident missionary to the Grand River in 1823 (SPG 1823:145). In 1828 the New England Company missionary, Mr. Lugger, took over the mission from the SPG. Lugger established several new schools, and worked on a Mohawk Grammar with Brant. Lugger did attempt to convert Indians from the other Nations, but one of the Delaware and Cayuga chiefs responded that, although they were in friendly alliance with the King, they did not feel it was right to change their religion (NEC 1829:9-10). By 1828, however, there were fifty Delawares requesting education, and the Tuscaroras had asked for a resident missionary. Lugger reported (Sept. 14, 1828) that he had been down to the mouth of the river with Brant, visiting the Six Nations, and that he had found the Onondagas and Delawares anxious for education, and prepared to build two schoolhouses with a place of worship attached, and the Oneida school was in very satisfactory condition. Lugger recommended Abraham Nelles as missionary for the Tuscaroras. In 1829, there were four schoolhouses, each with a lot of 100 acres attached, which the Indians had granted to the New England Company. At this time the SPG made over the Six Nations mission to the care of the New England Company (NEC 1829:11-14). The New England Company also started a small mission at Mud Lake in 1828.

The Mohawks were given money by the SPG on their settlement at the Bay of Quinte, to build a church, and this was completed in 1794. They were visited by the Rev. John Stuart from Kingston, twice a year. He found a schoolteacher for them, but in 1803 the teacher was dismissed because there were too few pupils. In 1812, John Stuart was succeeded by his son, George Okill Stuart, who continued to visit Tyendinaga for many years.

Methodists

a) Conversions

In 1822 the members of the Methodist Episcopal Church in the state of New York decided to send a missionary to the Six Nations Indians in Canada. Alvin Torry arrived at the Grand River in 1822, and in his journal described how he began his work by trying to "get acquainted with the history of the Six Nations, by attending their councils, and visiting them from house to house, and when opportunity offered, singing and praying with them" (Torry 1864:68). At first he had no success with the Indians, but held a camp meeting with neighbouring whites near the reservation, hoping it would attract the Indians. The Indians, however, avoided the whites, but attending the meeting were Peter and Polly Jones, who were the children of a Welsh surveyor and a Mississauga woman, and who had been brought up among the Six Nations Indians. Peter and Polly Jones were converted at the meeting, and when they returned to their home in the north part of the Mohawk settlement, they began to talk with and pray for their neighbours. By the time Torry went to the settlement, a number of Indians were interested in salvation. Torry began to hold meetings at the house of Thomas Davis, a Mohawk chief who was a baptized member of the Church of England, but was glad to have Torry preach to his people. At the first meeting, between twenty and thirty people were received into the church. They began to build a church and employed a schoolteacher. Thomas Davis became a Methodist.

Not long after his conversion, Torry writes, Peter Jones went to the Credit and persuaded his mother and the Indians, with their chief, Captain John, to visit the Grand River. Thirty of the Mississaugas were converted, and accepted an offer from the Mohawks to let them stay and till the land so that the children could attend the school. By 1825, there were over 150 converted Mississaugas, and they began to think of returning to the Credit. The Indians had never lived on their reserve at the Credit longer than to receive their annuities, because, as one of the best salmon fisheries on Lake Ontario, it had been occupied by white men for a long time. They petitioned the Government for the right of possession, and returned to the Credit and built a village in April, 1826 (1864:123).

Meanwhile, Peter Jones and the head of the Canada Conference of the Methodist Episcopal Church, Elder William Case, were concerned with the conversion of other Indians in this area. The next group of Indians to become converted were Mississaugas in the Belleville-Kingston area. The entry in Peter Jones' diary for February 17, 1826, describes a meeting with about a dozen Ojibwa who came thirty miles to hear what he had to say. Three days later he asked them what they thought of the things they had heard and whether they would like to become Christians, and they answered that they would, and would be glad to do better (Jones 1860: 57). On May 31, 1826, twenty-two converts of the Mississauga Indians were baptized and formed into a society at Belleville under the care of two of their principal men as leaders, William Beaver and John Sunday. Case reported that great changes had already taken place, and that more than forty people had already given up drinking, and that three times a day prayers could be heard in their wigwams. (MM 1826:310)

A camp meeting was held in June, 1826, on the Bay of Quinte, and the Indians were encouraged to attend. Case described it as follows:

> We were now informed the Mississauga fleet was in sight.
> . . . We found between 50 and 60 landing from their bark canoes.
> Their furniture of cooking utensils, guns, spears, etc., were taken
> out, with barks for covering their wigwams, their blankets rolled
> up, and all prepared to be borne on the heads of the squaws. When
> all were in readiness, the Indians took each a canoe, reversed,
> upon his head, — the squaws in the rear, — and the whole body
> advanced in Indian file to the encampment. . . . The number of
> adults which occupied this camp was 41; their children about 17;
> in all 58. Of the adults, about 28 had given evidence of a change
> of heart, two of whom officiated as exhorters. . . . (MM 1826:394-6)

During the camp meeting, twenty-one adults were baptized. "During these exercises their minds were considerably affected, and some of them so much as to be unable to stand, and were borne from the altar in the arms of their friends." Ten children were also baptized, so that by the end of the meetings, the total number of converts was forty-three adults and twenty-one children (MM 1826:394-6). During 1827 these Indians settled on twenty acres on Grape Island in the Bay of Quinte, and this settlement attracted Indians from the surrounding area; for instance, forty Indians came from Kingston after being converted (WAR 1827:7).

The people of Rice Lake also became interested in Christianity, in 1826. They heard of the conversions among the Belleville people, and wanted to see for themselves what it was all about. At the beginning of September, 1826, about twenty of them accompanied one of their chiefs to Hamilton (now Cobourg) to the annual meeting of the Conference. Case described the occasion:

> . . . These attended daily at the chapel, where they heard the word expounded, and as often assembled in their encampment to hear the word from Peter Jones and others of the native exhorters . . . Sept. 2 . . . their hearts appeared to melt, and they fell upon their knees and wept and prayed for mercy, while their converted brethren surrounded them in prayer and made supplication in their behalf. By the dusk of evening the whole number from Rice Lake, professed to obtain mercy of the Lord, and signified their purpose to renounce their pagan customs and follow the Lord . . . And their deportment since has evinced the sincerity of their profession. For on their return to their homes, they in a public and ceremonious manner cast away their "medicine bags". They have also renounced intoxication and everywhere are known to be a praying people. (CA & J, April 14, 1827:186)

A number of Indians from Rice Lake attended the quarterly meeting for the Rice Lake circuit on January 13, 1827 (CA & J, April 7, 1827:114). In May, 1827, meetings were held at Hamilton with about 100 Indians. According to Case, all of these people professed to renounce their "habits of paganism and intemperance", and about half of them had received baptism on a profession of faith in Christ at the meetings in January. On this occasion, forty-three more were baptized, twenty-seven of whom were over the age of ten. Some of the people had been converted at the meetings held there the previous September, but had not been baptized. Among the converts was the chief, George Paudash (CA & J, May 5, 1827: 137).

The Ojibwa Indians of Lake Simcoe were also approached by missionaries in 1826. In August, Peter Jones, with five other converted Indians, went to Holland Landing where the Indians of the Lake Simcoe area were gathered to receive their annual presents from the Government, and held meetings. There were about 600 Indians there, many of whom were drunk. After Peter Jones had spoken to the Indians, the Indian agent, Colonel Givins, expressed his approval of what Peter Jones had said, telling the Indians it was all truth, and he hoped they would think of it.

The Lake Simcoe Indians were divided into three groups: Yellowhead's people, Aisance's people, and Snake's people.

> The principal chief was consulted on the subject of Christianity; as was also the next senior chief. The former said the Indians could do as they thought best; as for himself, he had not made up his mind on the subject. He would think about it till next spring. The other said he would be glad to be instructed; he would come to the Credit soon, and perhaps leave some of his boys at the school. No opposition was expressed by any of them; and we judged that the prospects were favourable. (WAR 1826:19-20)

These expectations were fulfilled because the next annual report records that the head chief of the Simcoe Indians came to solicit a missionary, and said his people were willing to help support one (WAR 1827:3).

At a Council of the Chippewas on July 20, 1827, Yellowhead expressed his views:

> Our Native brothers are desirous of forming a settlement. . . . It is our desire to come together; many of us have thrown aside our former habits, and wish to adopt the habits of civilized life, to become Christians, and to worship which is known to the white's in the Good Book. . . . we shall then be enabled to pursue a regular system of agriculture, and greater facilities will be afforded us in following the precepts of our religious teachers. Those that have embraced Christianity already feel its happy effects. . . . (AT 1834:17).

Although the Methodists were having such success among the Indians of this area, their attempts to convert the Indians of southwestern Ontario were not meeting with success. At Munceytown, reception to the Methodists was mixed. The first attempt to civilize the Indians was made in 1825 by John Carey, a schoolteacher who went to Munceytown and offered to become a teacher there. Some of the Indians were in favour, and others were against the proposal. Chief Westbrook was among those in favour, and Carey decided to start a school (MM 1826:36-39). In May, 1825, Peter Jones and Alvin Torry visited Muncey where they spoke in council to George Turkey's people and to the Indians of Lower Muncey and the Ojibwa camp of Otemekoo, urging them to accept Christianity. At Otemekoo's camp the Indians said they could not give an answer as many of their chiefs and men were absent, but that they would think about it; they had a religion of their own, and it was the white people who made them drunk (Jones 1860:28-9). At the Upper Muncey village the four chiefs were divided, but Westbrook and Turkey were in favour of having a teacher; two said that the white man had cheated them out of their lands, and they would have nothing to do with him or his religion (Torry 1864:117). By 1829, the Methodists were only able to report ten conversions, and Case described Muncey as the most unpromising of their missions (CA & J, Feb. 19, 1830:97).

Peter Jones, with a party of Methodist Indians, visited the Indians of Lake St. Clair and Walpole Island in 1829. He spoke first to the St. Clair Indians under Chief Wawanosh who said they could not give an answer until the matter was brought before their head chief who lived on Walpole Island (Jones 1860:245). On their arrival at Walpole Island they found most of the Indians drunk, but the head chief, Pazhekezhikquashkum, was perfectly sober and agreed to summon all his people to listen to them the next morning. At noon all the principal men, about thirty of them, assembled. Brother Smith spoke, then Peter Jones described the conversion and happiness of the Indians in the east. Pazhekezhikquashkum welcomed them and said:

> . . . Brothers and friends, the Great Spirit made us all; he made the white man, and he made the Indian. When the Great Spirit made the white man he gave him his worship, written in a book, and prepared a place for his soul in heaven above. He also gave him his mode of preparing and administering medicine to the sick different from that of the Indians. Brothers and Friends, when the Great Spirit made the Indian he gave him his mode of worship, and the manner of administering and using medicine to the sick. The Great Spirit gave the Indian to know the virtue of roots and plants to preserve life; and by attending to these things our lives are preserved.

He went on to tell the story of Indians at the Miami who threw away their medicine bags and became Christians, and shortly afterwards became sick and died. He pointed out that only the day before, two white Christians had got drunk and fought on the Island. Why should they abandon the ways their Munedoo Spirit had appointed their forefathers to do and observe, when the white men were just as wicked as the Indians? Peter Jones was informed that "Chief Pazhekezhikquashkum is a great powwow, and that it was by his witchcraft he maintained his authority" (Jones 1860:246-9). As the Indians were afraid of offending him, it was only natural that he should try to prevent their accepting Christianity.

The missionaries met with more success with the Saugeen Indians who were first visited by the Indian speakers, Thomas McGee and John Thomas. In the summer of 1829, Peter Jones went to Saugeen and found about twenty-five Indians living in two camps; stayed with the Indians for two days and held several meetings. They had already heard from Thomas Big Canoe and Alexander Chief about what was happening at the Credit and Lake Simcoe, and were prepared for the reception of Christianity. They were attentive, and several of them wept and tried to call on the name of the Lord. Peter Jones spent a day explaining the Christian religion to the Chief Keketoonce who responded:

Brothers! I have listened to your words. I believe what you say. I will take your advice and worship with you in the Christian religion.

Brothers! I thank you for telling me the words of the Great Spirit. I thank you for remembering me, a poor, wretched and lonesome man. I have heard from afar that all my brethren around me are turning to the service of the Great Spirit, and forsaking their old religion. I do not wish to stand alone. Brothers! I will arise and follow them. I will be a Christian. It may be while I stretch out my hands to the Great Spirit for the blessings which my Christian brethren enjoy, I may receive a handful of the same before I die. . . .

Brothers! Becoming a Christian I shall desire to see my children read the good book. As for myself, I am too old to learn; and if I can only hear my children read, I shall be satisfied with what I hear from them.

Brothers! I shall tell all my young men your words — that I shall obey your instructions and become a Christian. It shall also be my desire to have my people settle where we may learn to serve the Great Spirit, and till the ground.

When Peter Jones' party left, they left the chief's son, Thomas Big Canoe, with the people, so he could give them instruction (CA & J, Feb. 5, 1830:94).

The Methodists also tried to start a mission among the Mohawks of the Bay of Quinte. On his way to the Mohawk settlement on February 16, 1826, Peter Jones received this letter:

To Mr. W. Case, Mohawk Village, Feb. 15th, 1826.

Sir, Being informed that a Peter Jones would wish to preach in this place, we would observe that we have no desire to hear him, or run after any new fangled doctrine, but intend to keep to that Church whose ministers first sounded the tidings of salvation in the forests of our forefathers, and turned them from the errors of their ways to the knowledge of the only true God; whom we still wish to worship in the way wherein we have been instructed, and to continue in the things which we have learned, and have been of, knowing of whom we have learned them and beg to subscribe ourselves . . . .
P.S. Such we believe is the wish of all the Mohawks in this place. (Jones 1860:56-57)

Peter Jones went on anyway and held a meeting; Abraham Hill joined the Methodists and later wrote to Colonel Givins to complain that many of his nation had used threatening words to him, saying that the King did not like the Methodists and would drive them all away from their lands (Jones 1860:189). In 1829, the Methodists reported thirty-three communicants (CA & J, May 15, 1829:145).

b) Church Organization

By 1829, the Methodists had flourishing church organizations at several places. At the Six Nations, Torry had established a mission among the Oneidas in 1827. The establishment of the schoolhouse at the Salt Springs among the Upper Mohawks had met with some opposition from the other Mohawks associated with the Church of England, who were afraid this would damage their standing with the Government. (RG10, vol. 441, Brant to Claus, May 27, 1826) Torry had also started appointments at Big Creek and the Cayuga village. By 1828 Messmore reported that there were ninety-five Indians in the church, and that the schools were in a prosperous state. (CA & J, Oct. 3, 1828:18)

In April, 1826, the Credit Indians moved to the Credit and built a village with a chapel and a school. In September, 1826, they received a missionary, Egerton Ryerson. Ryerson and Peter Jones divided the Indians into classes and selected two of the most pious and experienced men to be in charge of each class. Each class met once a week, and the leaders met with Ryerson every Sabbath. Early in 1827, there were 120 members in society (MM 1827:313-5); when James Richardson took over the mission in September, 1827, he found about 200 Indians living in twenty-two log houses. They had about half an acre attached to each house, fenced and cultivated, and a field of about thirty acres on the flats of the river, of which each family had its portion. The boys' school was taught by John Jones (Peter Jones' brother), and a school for girls was opened. It was built by the Indians, who also helped to build the missionary's house (CA & J, Jan. 11, 1828: 14). On January 1, 1829, the Indians appointed their road masters, constables, chapel keeper and collectors for the year, and Peter Jones was named a chief in the tribe. The council also considered the erection of a sawmill, and the building of a workshop and a hospital (Jones 1860:193-4). A hospital and a mechanic's shop were built during the year (WAR 1828-9:4).

Grape Island also became an important "model" community for the Methodists. William Case, the Elder of the Canada Conference, was the missionary. By July, 1827, the population had grown to about 160 people. Fifteen acres of land had been planted, a schoolhouse built, and six houses were being built. The mission supported a schoolteacher and a man to teach farming, whose wife taught the women knitting and sewing. Peter Jones divided the congregation into classes with leaders in 1828 (Jones 1860:102), and the Indians built a hospital and a school for girls (CA & J, Nov. 2, Nov. 25, 1828:54, 74). By 1829, there were 220 Indians at Grape Island, of whom 125 were regular communicants, and there were fifty-six children in the schools (CA & J, May 15, 1829:145). The Indians had built a work-house where they could work at trades, and some were learning shoemaking, joinery and cabinet work (Landon 1930: 475).

At Rice Lake, Case employed a teacher and made arrangements for a schoolhouse to be built, and the Indians promised to leave their women and children behind during the winter hunting season. By May, 1828, there were sixty scholars (MM 1828:387). Mr. Scott of the New England Company petitioned the Governor in 1828 for a plot of land near the mouth of the Otonabee River, of 1120 acres, and the Indians were given a license of occupation (NEC 1829:20). The Methodist mission moved on to Spook Island in Rice Lake where the schools were carried on. The missionary had 275 people under religious instruction and 175 of these were communicants (CA & J, May 15, 1829:145).

At Lake Simcoe, the Methodists had set up two schools by 1828, one at Holland Landing and the other on an Island at the Narrows. In 1829 the missionary reported 429 Indians under his tuition, 350 of whom were members of the church. There were 100 children in the two schools (CA & J, May 15, 1829:145). In July, 1829, Peter Jones found at Snake's Island, "the chief, Wm. Snake and his people, much engaged in religion"

(CA & J, Feb. 5, 1830:89), and they helped the missionary put up a schoolhouse and a house for the schoolteacher. At the Narrows at Yellowhead's Island they had a number of meetings "favoured with the divine spirit" (CA & J, Feb. 5, 1830:89), and helped build a schoolhouse. At Matchedash he described John Aisance and his people as "truly happy in religion. Although they have been converted scarcely a year, they have gained considerable knowledge of the Christian religion for the time." (CA & J, Feb. 5, 1830:89). They had planted about twenty acres in corn and potatoes, and built a home for the schoolteachers.

> The chief takes a deep interest in the welfare of his people, and is much pleased with the prospects of a school. He is a sensible man and exhorts his people powerfully. This people are much devoted to the service of God. There have been no instances of intoxication among them since their conversion. The leaders are very vigilant in the discharge of their duty. (CA & J, Feb. 5, 1830:89)

Summary

Between 1784 and 1830, the Indians lost most of their land and became dependent on the Government, although at this stage the Government did not intervene in the internal affairs of the groups. In 1822 Methodist missionaries came from the United States and made many converts and established settled communities among the previously itinerant Mississauga and Lake Simcoe groups. Missionaries were not so successful further west among the other Ojibwa groups. It seems that the Indians who had the most contact with whites were the most receptive to Christianity, and this and other factors are discussed in the last chapter. Methodism made a great impact on the Mississauga groups, both spiritually and socially, and the missionaries were much encouraged by their success in creating "model" Christian peasant communities. Their success encouraged the Government to try to emulate their methods and to introduce the policies that are discussed in the next chapter.

CHAPTER III

MISSION WORK EXPANDS

Between 1828 and 1829 the Government and the officers of the military in Upper Canada seriously evaluated the role and condition of the Indian Department. This was the prelude to a new approach to Indian affairs and the year 1830 marked the beginning of a new era in Indian-Government relations, as Sir John Colborne decided to involve the Government in the civilization of the Indians through the establishment of model communities. The Government encouraged British Wesleyan Methodist and Church of England missionaries to come and counteract the influence of the American Methodists.

This chapter opens with a discussion of the policies and philosophies of the Government and the missionary societies; it is important to understand the political context at the national level because prevailing antagonistic or sympathetic relations between the Government and missionary societies had a considerable effect on the attitudes of Indians, agents and missionaries towards each other at the local level. The mission work in the local communities is then described to provide a spatial and chronological context for reference in the following discussion of the roles of the missionaries, and to illustrate some of the processes of change.

In 1830 there was a revision of the policies and structure of the Indian Department. Darling commented on the work of the missionaries in civilizing the Indians, and suggested that the encouragement of civilization by the Government would be the best way of maintaining the Indians as allies to the Crown (AT 1834:29). The Secretary of State for the colonies was anxious to cut down the expenses of the Indian Department, but Sir James Kempt, Commander of the Forces, argued that this would reduce the efficiency of the Department, and compromise their faith with the Indians. It was his opinion that:

> As allies, the Indians are wasteful and expensive, consuming great quantities of stores, procured with difficulty, and which might be far more beneficially applied; but their barbarous treatment of prisoners and wounded men, makes it impolitic to provoke their

hostility; and so long as they retain their habits of savage life, and their alliance in war is considered important, the department and the issue of presents must, however modified, be continued. . . .
In conclusion, it appears that the most effectual means of ameliorating the condition of the Indians, of promoting their religious improvement and education, and of eventually relieving His Majesty's Government from the expense of the Indian Department are:
1st. To collect the Indians in considerable numbers and to settle them in villages, with a due portion of land for their cultivation and support.
2nd. To make such provision for their religious improvement, education and instruction in husbandry, as circumstances may from time to time require.
3rd. To afford them such assistance in building their houses, rations, and in procuring such seed and agricultural implements as may be necessary, commuting when practicable, a portion of their presents for the latter.
4th. To provide active and zealous missionaries for the Indians at the Bay of Quinte and Gwillimburg; and to send Wesleyan missionaries from England to counteract the antipathy to the established church and other objectionable principles which the Methodist missionaries from the United States are supposed to instil into the minds of their Indian converts. (AT 1834:39, 41)

Sir James Kempt suggested that the Indian Department should be divided into four districts, each under a superintendent, and it was suggested by Sir John Colborne (May 7, 1829) that Col. Givins should be Chief Superintendent, Anderson in charge of the Matchedash and Lake Simcoe Indians, Ironside at the River Thames and St. Clair, Captain Brant at the Six Nations, and Clench for the Mohawks and Mississaugas of the Bay of Quinte and Rice Lake. The duties of the superintendents would include gathering the Indians together into villages, persuading them to cultivate the land, establishing schools, leasing lands, and purchasing cattle and agricultural implements, etc. (AT 1834:41).

Sir John Colborne reported in 1830 on the success of his work:

. . . I beg leave to state to you the measures which have been this year adopted to carry into effect the system recommended to be pursued, with a view to introducing amongst the Indians of Upper Canada, the industrious habits of civilized life. The three tribes residing on the shores of Lake Simcoe, and near the Matchadash, and the Potaganasees from Drummond Island, have been placed under charge of a superintendent of the Indian department, and urged to clear a tract of land between the Lakes Huron and Simcoe.

I have directed houses to be built for them on detached lots, and they are now clearing ground sufficient to establish farms at each station for their immediate support, from which they will be supplied while they are bringing into cultivation their individual lots marked out for their residence. Agricultural implements have been procured for them, experienced farmers have been engaged to instruct them, and school masters appointed to educate their children. I have taken steps also to establish a school at which a certain number from each tribe in Canada may receive an education that will qualify them in a few years to become teachers.

The Western Indians, and those from the northern shore of Lake Huron, who repair annually to this quarter to receive their presents, will, I hope, be prevailed on to abandon, gradually, their present mode of life, and to follow the example of the Indians at these stations, when they see the advantages resulting from civilization.

Similar measures are on trial at the Indian stations on the Thames and Lake St. Clair. . . .   (AT 1834:128)

Colborne was very optimistic about the success of his plan, and looked to the long range goal, which, although involving considerable initial financing by the Government, would eventually mean financial independence for the Indian communities, relieving the Government of the expense of the Indian Department. Not only was Colborne practical, but he was concerned with honour:

. . . The British Government cannot . . . get rid of an inconvenient debt, contracted at a period when an alliance with the Indians was highly appreciated.

The policy which it was considered prudent to countenance for the purpose of gaining their good opinion and respect is notorious, as well as the system of cringing flattery and fair promises which was pursued on all occasions when their active cooperation in support of British interests was necessary.

However embarrassing, therefore, it may be found to incur an expense annually for presents, I am persuaded . . . that this periodical acknowledgement of their claims and exertions cannot be discontinued without a loss of character on the part of the British nation. (AT 1834:141)

Colborne's plan was not supported with adequate finances by the Government, and with the replacement in 1836 of Colborne as Lieutenant-Governor of Upper Canada, by Sir Francis Bond Head, the policy changed. Head's sentiments about the Indians differed considerably from those of his predecessors. He stressed the simplicity of the Indians, and the harm that had been caused by the white man. He believed that they were dying out as a result of consumption and inter-breeding with whites. He concluded:

1. That an attempt to make Farmers of the Red Men has been, generally speaking, a complete Failure.
2. That congregating them for the Purpose of Civilization has implanted many more Vices than it has eradicated; and consequently;
3. That the greatest Kindness we can perform towards these intelligent, simple-minded People, is to remove and fortify them as much as possible from all Communication with the Whites. (BNA Provinces 1839:124)

He therefore proposed to settle as many of the Indians as possible on Manitoulin Island. He persuaded several groups of Indians to surrender tracts of land. With the proceeds of the sale of these lands, Head planned to defray the expenses of the Indian Department, and he justified his actions by claiming that the Indians were not naturally farmers, and the land of Manitoulin Island was more suited for their needs than that of southern Ontario. He was not in favour of cutting out the presents, because he did not see it as a long range problem, but he immediately stopped all the work of building at Manitoulin Island and dismissed all the people who had been hired.

We have only to bear patiently with them for a short Time, and with a few Exceptions, principally Half-castes, their unhappy Race, beyond our Power of Redemption, will be extinct. (BNA Provinces 1839:129)

The Secretary of State for the Colonial Department, Lord Glenelg, did not agree that the Indians could not be saved, but he agreed that they should be removed from white influences, and he concurred with Head's proposals.

In 1838, Sir Francis Bond Head resigned from the Government of Upper Canada, after the 1837 rebellion, and after this time the supervision and management of Indian Affairs came under the jurisdiction of the Chief Superintendent of Indian Affairs, Colonel Jarvis. The policies of Sir Francis Bond Head established a trend that was followed for many years.

The Missionaries

The Government invited the British Methodists to work in Upper Canada
in 1832 to counteract the influence of the American Methodists (BNA
Provinces 1829:90). The Canadian Conference amalgamated with the
British Conference in 1833, and Joseph Stinson took over from Case as
the General Superintendent. In 1834 the British Conference sent out
five new missionaries to the Indians: Jonathan Scott, Benjamin Slight,
John Douse, Jonathan Gladwin, and William Steer (Findlay and Holdsworth 1921:461-462).

The missionaries could not agree with Sir Francis Bond Head that the
Indians were incapable of improvement, and the General Secretary of
the Wesleyan Missions in Britain expressed his views in a letter to Lord
Glenelg, December 14, 1837. He also recommended that the Government should secure by a grant the Indian reservations and make them
inalienable without the joint agreement of the Lieutenant-Governor, the
principal Chief of the settlement and the resident missionary. Because
the Indians did not have title deeds, they were very insecure and believed that if they made any improvements, the land would soon be
taken away from them. He thought they should also have a right to vote
(BNA Provinces 1839:90-98).

The Ministers of the Canadian Conference also tried to influence the
Government in a memorial to Sir Francis Bond Head. They pointed out
the state of dissatisfaction existing among the Indians in some of their
mission stations, because they had no title deeds and no security. The
Indians had been persuaded to surrender lands; in the case of the Saugeen Indians they were not at the disposal of the people who surrendered them; in another case they had made improvements on lands granted
by Sir John Colborne, and had then been scattered in the wilderness
(BNA Provinces 1839:152-3). Sir Francis Bond Head was offended by
this memorial, and said that dissatisfaction existed only on the Methodist stations, and that therefore the Methodists must have caused it. He
dismissed as ridiculous the idea that the Indians wanted title deeds:

> The Methodist Ministers might just as well declare, that when
> wild Beasts roar at each other it is to complain of the Want
> among them of Marriage Licences, for Animals understand
> these *"Documents"* just as well as Indians understand Title
> Deeds. (BNA Provinces 1839:249)

The idea that the Methodists should act as trustees for the Indian land appalled him. He said that they were supporters of his Government, but that:

> ... the Blow which the Rev. Egerton Ryerson, by his late Mis-representations in England, successfully struck at the Legislative Council of this Province, has evidently induced him ... to try the same Experiment upon me. ... I was ready to attack either the Instant they should presume to meddle with the Duties of my station. (BNA Provinces 1839:152)

He warned the Methodists against interfering in political matters, and also warned them:

> "The strong Feeling of Dissatisfaction" which you assure me exists among the Indians should warn you of the Danger of the Arrangement you propose; for if such a Feeling can insidiously be implanted in the Minds of this virtuous Race against the Acts of the Representative of a Sovereign whose disinterested Gener-osity to the Indians cannot be unknown to you, how severely might it be made to fall upon any Band of Christian Ministers who, unmindful of the Admonitions of History, and regardless of the strong Feeling against Ecclesiastical Domination which exists in this noble Province, should be found connecting the temporal with the spiritual Management of their Flock? (BNA Provinces 1839:154)

In addition to their bad relationship with the Government, the Metho-dists suffered internal troubles with a split between the British and Canadian Conferences which lasted from 1841 to 1848.

The Church of England was supported by government policy, and John Strachan had great influence with the Government. However, al-though Strachan applied to the Church Missionary Society in 1829 for seven or eight missionaries to counteract the Methodist work, they did not send missionaries. The New England Company maintained mission-aries on the Grand River and at Mud Lake. The Company itself was non-sectarian, but the missionaries took spiritual support from the Church of England Bishop of the diocese. The Company was also non-political:

> The direction contained in the Charter under which they act is general, "to instruct the Indians in the Knowledge of the true and only God, and in the Protestant Religion". There is in the Con-stitution of the New England Company nothing of a Political Nature. ... (BNA Provinces 1839:115)

In 1830, a missionary society was formed in Toronto for Converting and Civilizing the Indians, and Propagating the Gospel among Destitute

Settlers in Upper Canada. The society supported a travelling missionary in the Coldwater district from 1833 to 1835, and another missionary at Caradoc from 1835 to 1838, at which date the society disappeared (Waddilove 1838, and Annual Reports).

The Church Missionary Society supported a missionary at Sarnia from 1868 to 1870. The SPG supported the missionary on Walpole Island from 1841 until 1885. Church of England missions were not very widespread during the period.

The Moravians maintained missionaries at New Fairfield during the period, though their missions suffered various setbacks. Two new arrivals on the scene in the 1840's were the Baptists, who came from the U.S.A. to establish a mission at Tuscarora, and later at Oneida, and the Roman Catholics, who established a mission on Walpole Island and attempted to set up another one at Sarnia. Both met with opposition from the other missionaries, and the Catholics were forced to withdraw.

The Local Communities

In the following section an outline of some of the events in the local communities is given to illustrate the progress and general characteristics of the mission work. Unfortunately, the amount of information available for each community varies considerably, and significant events are often few and far between; inconsistency is inevitable. The order in which the communities are described is based partly on the denomination with which the community was first affiliated, and partly on geographical location.

The first category of communities includes those that converted to Methodism in the 1820's, and remained Methodist without any challenge from other denominations. For the most part they were composed of Mississauga Indians under one chief, or united leadership. They were located in the eastern section of the area, and include the Credit, Grape Island, Rice Lake and Lake Scugog. (See map, p. 30.)

The Credit — New Credit

The Methodist mission at the Credit prospered during the 1830's. In 1838 the missionary reported:

> The Indians of this mission have 820 acres of land in a state of cultivation, for the growth of provinder and grain, besides their gardens and there are nearly 20 of these adjoining their houses. . . .

They have 22 comfortable cottages . . . the side walks of the village are planked with thick boards . . . they have two stores in the village . . . seven barns, one blacksmith's shop, one carpenters shop, a parsonage house, a school house and a chapel. They have 200 shares in an excellent harbour on the Lake shore. . . . There are very few young people in the village but can read, write, and keep accounts . . . a third of the people are members of the church. . . . (MMN, Stinson, April 5, 1838)

The chiefs were anxious to get the title to their lands, but the pressure of white settlement was too great, and in 1847 the community moved to the Grand River (although Jarvis had tried to persuade them to move to Manitoulin Island). According to Peter Jones, the reasons for the move were the scarcity of wood, the need for a larger tract of land, they were surrounded by white people and the young people were tempted to drink, and the village arrangement was inconvenient for farming (CG, Jan. 12, 1848:49). At New Credit, the Indians were unsettled because of the problem with squatters, which discouraged them from cultivating their lands (WAR 1852:xiv). They were also without a resident missionary until 1852, at which time the missionary reported that their condition had improved slightly (WAR 1853:xiii).

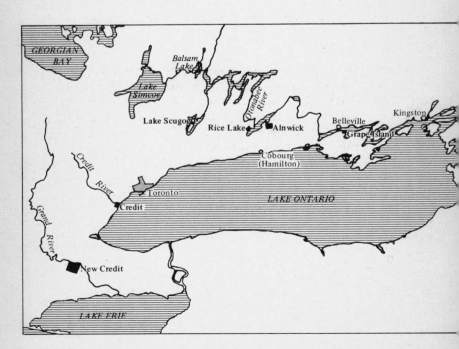

Grape Island – Alnwick

The people of Grape Island were very industrious during the 1830's; the Superintendent of Methodist missions commented on their "well-built little cottages, their highly cultivated gardens, their comfortable and neat clothing, and, above all, their peaceable and truly devotional religious exercises" (CG, Sept. 24, 1834:182). In 1837, the community moved to Aldersville, or Alnwick, on the south shore of Rice Lake, because it had expanded so much. They were assigned 3,400 acres of land, but were unsuccessful in attempts to get some form of title to the land. The tract was divided into fifty-acre lots, on which twenty-six frame houses and fourteen log houses were built. The move cost the community the blacksmith's and carpenter's shops, but the Methodists ran a manual labour school which combined elementary instruction with domestic economy. At the split between the English and Canadian Conferences in 1841, John Sunday, a chief and missionary, stayed with the English Methodists, his reason being the kindness of the English people which he had experienced on his trip to England (MMN, April 7, 1841). By the end of the 1850's, reports from the missionaries and the chiefs were discouraging, particularly about the generation gap. The young people preferred hunting to farming, and would not accept the authority of the council.

Rice Lake

By the beginning of 1830, the Indians were settled on 1100 acres of land granted them by the Government on the north shore of Rice Lake, with ninety members of the Methodist Church (CA & J, March 5, 1830: 106). The split between the Methodists caused some trouble – according to Peter Jones, the women supported the Canadian Conference, and the men went with the British Conference because it was "better liked by the Governor" (CG, Jan. 20, 1841:50). There was some pressure on the Indians in 1848 to move to Alnwick, and the consequent insecurity was not conducive to improvement of the land. However, the Indians remained at Rice Lake, and by 1858, there were 145 people.

Lake Scugog

By 1830, the Indians of Lake Scugog were mostly living at Mud Lake, but in 1835 they petitioned Sir John Colborne for a tract of land on Balsam Lake. They were granted a tract of 1206 acres of poor quality land. Forty-eight adults and forty-two children were involved in the move

(RG10, vol. 136, Jarvis to Governor General, May 24, 1843). The government agent was supposed to lay out lots of thirty acres and arrange for houses to be built, but, according to the Methodist missionary, instead of having ten comfortable cottages by 1839, they had only two log houses and six others partly built. The Methodist mission was supplied by a preacher from Peterborough (WAR 1839:17).

In 1843, the Indians bought 600 acres on Lake Scugog as they were dissatisfied with the climate and land at Balsam Lake. At first they worked enthusiastically at clearing and cultivating the land, but failure to sell their improvements at Balsam Lake, or to get attention from the government agents who were pressuring them to move to Rice Lake, discouraged their efforts. By 1858 there were only sixty-one people in the band, and only twelve children of school age; there was no resident schoolmaster or missionary (CR 1858:87).

Lake Simcoe

The Lake Simcoe groups that are described next were also converted to Methodism in the 1820's, but in 1830 they were involved in a government settlement scheme, in the operation of which they were exposed to Church of England and Catholic missionaries and government agents. By the end of the period, the settlement had split up and the Indians moved to Rama, Beausoleil Island, and Snake Island. This was a test case and its failure spelt the failure of all government schemes. (See map, p. 33.)

In 1830 the three groups of the Lake Simcoe area and the Potaganasee* people from Drummond Island were placed under the charge of a superintendent of the Indian Department, and urged to clear a tract of land between Lake Simcoe and Lake Huron. A village was built for Yellowhead's and Snake's people at the Narrows of Lake Simcoe, and another village was built for John Aisance's people and the Potaganasees at Matchedash Bay. The plan was to build a seminary at Matchedash. The Methodists had missionaries with all three of the Lake Simcoe groups, and the Potaganasees were Roman Catholic.

The plans did not run smoothly. The Church of England priest at Matchedash was opposed to any Methodist or Roman Catholic competition in his work (RG10, Vol. 5, Archbold to Colborne, Aug. 23, 1830). At both places the Indians refused to live exactly where the superintendent wanted them to. In October, the establishment at Matchedash was

*Probably Potawatomi.

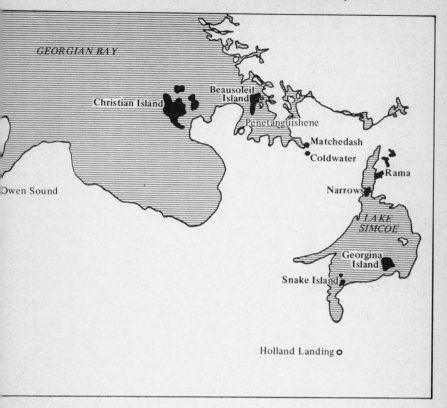

moved to Coldwater. During 1831, at the Narrows, there was a bitter
quarrel between the farmer who was employed by the Government and
a member of the Church of England, and the Methodist missionaries;*
this affected the progress of the work, though it is difficult to estimate
to what extent the Indians were directly involved. At Coldwater, Chief
Aisance quarrelled with the Methodist minister, who was forced to leave,
and Aisance became a Catholic, along with three of his people (RG10,
Vol. 49, Anderson to Givins, Dec. 12, 1831; Vol. 51, Currie to Richardson, April 16, 1832, Anderson).

By September, 1832, the agent was trying to find ways of reducing
the expenses of the establishment, and decided to cut down on the staff;

*There is a large volume of correspondence on this subject in the Christian Guardian,
1832, and RG10, vols. 48, 50.

the houses had not been finished (RG10, Vol. 51, Anderson to Givins, Sept. 17, 1832). The scheme was generally considered a failure, and in 1836, Sir Francis Bond Head suggested that the Indians would be better off if they sold their depleted hunting grounds, rather than staying on them surrounded by the white population. The chiefs decided to accept the offer, and in 1838 the settlements dissolved (BNA Provinces 1839: 150-1). Yellowhead's people went to Rama, Aisance's people to Beausoleil Island, and Snake's people returned to Snake Island in Lake Simcoe.

Rama

Between 1843 and 1848, Yellowhead's Indians bought 1,600 acres at Rama out of their own funds (CR 1858:82). The Methodist missionary reported a conflict between Chief Yellowhead and his subordinate chiefs, and in 1845, the chief left the Methodist Church and joined the Church of England. Yellowhead's request for a Church of England church was refused by the Governor, who told him to stick with the church of their first choice (WAR 1845:xv). The division between Methodists and Church of England members continued for some years, based on Yellowhead's opposition to the Methodists and his personal influence, but the Church of England did not seriously challenge the Methodist mission.

Beausoleil – Christian Island

In 1842, 232 Indians from Coldwater settled on Beausoleil Island. Many of the Indians were Roman Catholics, but the Methodists maintained a connection from Rama, with a membership of thirty-eight in 1847 (WAR 1847:xv). As early as 1848, the chiefs were looking for a place to call their own, and were considering Christian Island, but they did not move there until 1858. There were already ninety-four Potawatomies and Ottawas living on Christian Island, but the Beausoleil Indians offered to take them into the Band and share the annuities if they would become Christians. The Ottawas were mostly Roman Catholics who had migrated to Christian Island in 1854 (CR 1858:83-84). During the 1860's the Methodists maintained a missionary who visited Christian Island, Beausoleil Island, where there were still a few families, and French River. The Roman Catholics were visited by a priest from Penetanguishene.

Snake Island – Georgina Island

The Indians returned to Snake Island in 1839. These islands had never been surrendered to the Crown. They were visited occasionally by the Methodist missionary from Rama, and in 1841 a schoolteacher was hired who also acted as local preacher (WAR 1841:13). There were 109 people at Snake Island in 1842, but in 1843 the Indians were often away hunting, leaving the school deserted. In 1845, therefore, the mission was included in the Newmarket circuit, leaving a schoolteacher resident at Snake Island. During the 1860's, the people began to move to Georgina Island, and by 1866, there were about fifteen families on each island. During the 1870's, most of the remaining people moved to Georgina Island (WAR 1867:xxiii; 1879:xix).

The next set of communities to be described resisted conversion in the 1820's, and became part of the Government's settlement scheme in 1830. The Methodists did the initial work in these communities, but usually more than one denomination was involved in attempts to convert the Indians, and the story of their association with missionaries and government agents becomes more complicated. Geographically, the order followed moves from the Thames region (Muncey and Oneida), to the Lake St. Clair region (Sarnia), up the shore of Lake Huron to the Saugeen Peninsula (Saugeen and Newash). Moraviantown is in this geographical area with Muncey and Oneida, but as a Moravian mission is in a class by itself in other respects. The Wyandots of Amherstburg are also in a class by themselves. (See map, p. 36.)

Munceytown

In 1829 a village was laid out at Muncey, and houses and a schoolhouse built (WAR 1829-31:6). J.B. Clench was appointed the resident Superintendent.

Peter Jones went to Muncey in April, 1830, to work with the Indians. In a council held by Clench and the Chippewa and Munsee chiefs and principal men, the agent told the Indians that the Government wished them to become Christians, as well as civilized. The Munsees replied that they had not committed themselves to becoming Christians until they found out whether the Government wished them to become Christian. He said that they would accept Christianity, but keep their own religion too (RG10, Vol. 5, Peter Jones, May 25, 1830). The Chippewa Indians said they could not make up their minds without consulting the chiefs at the St. Clair River. Of sixty-six converts reported for April, 1830, eleven

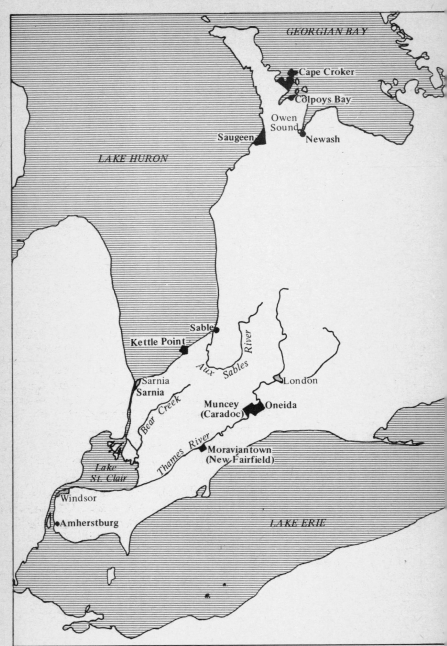

were Munsees and fifty-five Chippewa (CG, May 8, 1830:197). The Government was attempting to settle many of the Ojibwa groups at Colborne, and Clench managed to persuade the Bear Creek Chippewa to settle on the Thames (RG10, Vol. 50, Clench to Givins, March 14, 1832).

In 1835, the Rev. Richard Flood of the Church of England began to visit the Munsee and Chippewa Indians. Methodist work was progressing with 157 members (WAR 1835:5) among the Chippewa, and Flood decided to visit the Bear Creek and Munsee Indians (Waddilove 1838:125). Flood was fortunate to convert Captain Snake of the Munsees, who acted as interpreter and made sure the people went to church (Waddilove 1838:134).

The Methodists were established at Colborne with the Chippewas of the Thames and the Church of England was established at Lower Muncey with the Munsees and Bear Creek Chippewas. The bad feeling between the Bear Creek and Colborne Chippewas which persisted during the 1840's involved the missions to the extent that the Indians divided into parties which were associated with churches, and on both sides there were accusations that the missionaries were interfering with worldly matters and trying to stir up jealousy between the two bodies of Indians. The Chippewas could not agree over the division of the annuity, and who was the senior chief. The Munsees were also at odds with the Colborne Chippewas because they were restricted to one square mile of land, though they had often asked for more. The commissioners in the 1858 report thought that the Munsees were entitled to an equal share in the benefits from the land. In 1858 there were 340 Chippewas and 240 Munsees on the reserve (CR 1858:46-7).

Oneida

The Oneida Indians came from the United States in 1840, and settled on 5,000 acres which they bought in the township of Delaware. There were 436 people in the band (CR 1858:44). The Methodists reported that they had applied to the Wesleyan Methodist Conference for a missionary (WAR 1841:15), and by 1844 there were sixty-two Oneida in society* (WAR 1844:vii). In 1846, the Church of England started a mission on the reserve with Richard Flood. According to the Oneida chief, Moses Schuyler, all the people who applied to the Church of England had been dismissed from the Methodist Church for gross immorality (RG10, Vol. 441,

*A term used by the Methodists to refer to church members. See p. 54.

Schuyler to Flood, Sept. 27, 1846). By 1858, however, the Church of England mission had closed down, and the commissioners reported that the former Church of England Indians had "relapsed into Paganism". The population had increased to 529 by 1858 (CR 1858:45).

St. Clair

In 1827 the Ojibwa of the Lake St. Clair region surrendered 2,182,049 acres of land to the Crown for an annuity of $4,400, and the reserves of Sarnia, Kettle Point and Rive aux Sables, and Moore were set apart for them. In May, 1831, William Jones was appointed superintendent of the Sarnia reserve, and the Indians were collected together and houses built and lots laid out for them. The portion of the band who did not wish to be "civilized" settled at Walpole Island. In 1836, at a council, the annuity was officially divided between these two groups, and the reserve at Moore added to the Walpole Reserve (CR 1847, App. 21).

The first missionary to settle at Sarnia was Thomas Turner of the British Wesleyans in 1832. At his arrival the Indians were dispersed because of cholera, and it was not until May, 1833, that they moved into the houses the Government had built. In May, 1833, Peter Jones tried to form a society, but when James Evans took over the mission in July, 1834 (MMN, Turner, May 31, 1833), he found the Indians still opposed to Christianity, and drunk most of the time. By the beginning of March, 1835, Evans reported fifteen converts, including the head chief, Wawanosh, but little material improvement (CG, March 18, 1835:62).

In 1840, the interpreter, George Henry, quarrelled with the missionary, and threatened to join the Church of England. It was rumoured that Wawanosh had tried to get Henry out so he could appoint his son David as interpreter. In 1841 Wawanosh charged Keating (the agent for Walpole Island) with habitual intoxication and encouraging the Indians to drink, swearing, proselytizing for the Church of England, etc. Soon after this, charges were brought against Wawanosh by some of the Indians, supported by the agent, who accused him of mismanagement and improper conduct. The Methodist missionary, Scott, supported Wawanosh, but in 1843 Wawanosh was dismissed from his position, and Mishebishee was appointed in his place.

During 1844 and 1845, Roman Catholic missionaries attempted to establish a mission at Sarnia, and baptized some of the Indians, but they were forced to abandon their mission after trouble at Walpole Island.

In 1848, James Mishebishee resigned the chiefship in favour of Joshua

Wawanosh, and the council unanimously appointed David Wawanosh, who had been educated at Upper Canada College out of the band funds, as schoolteacher (RG10, Vols. 439, 436).

From 1868 to 1870, a missionary of the Church Missionary Society, Edmund Wilson, ran a mission at Sarnia. This is hardly mentioned in the Wesleyan reports (which illustrates the danger of relying on one version of historical events), although Wilson claimed that the old chief, Wawanosh, and twelve to fourteen families joined the Church of England. Wilson, however, mentioned that he met with much opposition from the Methodists at first (CMS 1868, Nov. 2).

At the Sable, the Indians had split with the Methodists in the 1840's, and invited a Church of England missionary to visit them. In the 1850's the Methodists worked again at the Sable, only to have the work challenged in 1868 by Wilson. After 1870, the Methodists regained control.

Saugeen

In 1831, the Methodists had established a mission at Saugeen. There were 177 people in the band, and of the forty members in society, thirty had been baptized before the mission was set up (WAR 1829-31:7-8). By 1836, there were sixty-three members in society.

In 1836, the Indians surrendered to Sir Francis Bond Head a tract of land containing about 1,600,000 acres, and reserved the Saugeen Peninsula with about 450,000 acres (Copway 1847:215). After this surrender, the Indians divided into two bands, one at Saugeen and the other at Newash, or Owen's Sound (CR 1858:74).

In 1843, George Copway was appointed missionary at Saugeen, and reported favourably on the material and spiritual state of the community. By 1846, Saugeen was visited occasionally by missionaries from Owen Sound. During the next few years there was conflict among the chiefs. David Sawyer, an Indian who was missionary at Owen Sound and did agent's work for the Indians, was a subject of controversy. In 1854, the Indians surrendered the Saugeen Peninsula (see Appendix I). By 1858, there were 256 people in the community.

Newash (Big Bay, Owen's Sound)*

In 1841, the Indians at Big Bay, Owen Sound asked for a missionary

*Original way of referring to Owen Sound.

and schoolteacher, and during 1841, they were visited several times by the Methodist Indian missionary at Saugeen, and about twenty of them were converted (WAR 1841:17). In 1843, the Rev. Herkimer was missionary. There was conflict among the Indians at Newash in the 1840's. A number of Indians were dissatisfied with Chief Wabadick, and tried to get Peter Saco of Colpoy's Bay appointed chief. The Methodist missionary supported the opposition to the chief. In 1846, David Sawyer, who had been educated at the Grand River and was a local preacher for the Methodists, went to Owen Sound as schoolteacher, and was soon appointed as a chief and sat on the council. Sawyer and Wabadick did not get along. When Sawyer went to Saugeen in 1851, Charles Kezicks was appointed agent in his place. Wabadick then lost his position, and Kegedonce was appointed head chief. In 1852, a group of Indians with Kezicks, quarrelled with the Methodist missionary over the right to appoint the schoolmaster. Kezicks wanted to appoint Winter, who was a member of the Church of England. In 1853, Wabadick was reinstated, and apparently took the side of the Methodist missionary against the members of the Churches of Rome and England, who had decided to unite as a party. It was in 1852 that a resolution was taken in council at Saugeen to manage the affairs of the three bands in a general council, and Kegedonce accused Wabadick of resorting to this measure in order to gain a majority for the Methodists, who were in a minority at Newash. During 1854 and 1855, the factions were active in their quarrel (correspondence in RG10, vols. 129, 144, 139, 134, 133, 409, 410, 123, 412, 413, 411).

In 1854, the surrender of the Saugeen Peninsula occurred. The Methodist missionary, Conrad Van Dusen, was very unhappy with the terms of the surrender, and in his book, *The Indian Chief* (1867), he gives some of the reasons, which are quoted in Appendix I (see p. 93).

With the surrender of the land in 1854, the Newash Indians had reserved 15,586 acres at Cape Croker, laid out in farms of twenty-five acres to be given to each family with a licence of occupation. By 1858, Newash was no longer a mission, and the people were unenthusiastically preparing to move to Cape Croker. There were 238 people in the band (CR 1858:77-8).

Moraviantown (New Fairfield)

Col. Clench went to New Fairfield in 1835, and asked the Indians if they wanted to sell any of their land. They said they would exchange a tract of three square miles for a saw mill and a grist mill (MI, vol. 5, no. 7,

1835:290). In November, Brother and Sister Jesse Vogler joined the mission. In 1837, a large portion of the congregation left for the United States after a series of events that caused distress to the missionaries. According to the missionaries, Sir Francis Bond Head passed through New Fairfield in 1836, but instead of speaking with the missionaries, he arranged to meet some of the Indians. He then suggested they should move north or emigrate, and they could have all the land they wanted, or at least they should sell the portion of land on the north bank of the river for an annuity of $600. The Indians told the rest of the congregation, but most of them did not want to sell any land. However, a few who wanted to emigrate arranged secretly with the Lieutenant Governor to sell the land. Four weeks later, Clench came with a contract for the sale of the land on the north bank. A vote was taken, and the result was 28-26 in favour of the proposal. The missionaries finally agreed to sign if they could keep certain portions of the land. Terms were agreed upon, and the contract was signed (BNA Provinces 1839:105-6). The missionaries considered the proceedings illegal, as they considered themselves the trustees of the land.

In 1840, the Methodists at Muncey tried to settle and build a chapel, but were refused permission by the missionaries (MI, vol. 7, no. 12, 1842: 575). In 1846, a quarrel broke out between the missionaries and a group of Indians over the right to cut timber on the reserve, and the disaffected Indians had meetings with the Methodist preacher in George Snake's house. The Methodist faction was led by Chiefs Philip and Christian Jacobs (MI, Vol. 9, no. 5, 1847:195; RG10, Vol. 440, Vogler to Clench, Jan. 25, 1846). In 1857, the community was surveyed and divided into lots, and the community was spread out over the reserve instead of being grouped in a village (CR 1858:48-51). The lines of division into Methodist and Moravian parties became permanent. By 1866, the Anglican Church was also trying to gain a foothold on the reserve. By 1867, the groups were living peacefully on the reserve, and the Moravian missionaries had lost all their authority.

Wyandots of Amherstburg

The Methodist missionaries reported that there were forty Methodists (eighteen members) at Amherstburg during 1829-31 and the rest of the Indians were Roman Catholics (WAR 1829-31:6). The Indians were visited by preachers from Amherstburg.

The death of the chief, Francis Warron, in 1832, gave rise to problems, a group of Indians complaining that since then they had been under two chiefs who prevented them from improving their condition (RG10, vol. 52, Oct. 13, 1832). In 1833 the reserve was surrendered to the King in trust for the Indians. In 1836, two-thirds of the reserve were ceded, one-third of which was to be sold for "the benefit of Indians generally". There was great dissatisfaction among the Wyandots about the terms of this treaty (CR 1858:51).

During the 1840's there was considerable conflict between Chief Thomas Clarke and Chiefs Francis Park and John Hunt, but there is no suggestion that there was anything sectarian about the long-standing quarrels between the various chiefs. In the Commissioners Report for 1858, it is reported that there were sixty-five people on the reserve, of whom half were Methodists and the other half Roman Catholics.

The final category includes the communities that were primarily assoc-iated with the Church of England missionary societies. These communities are taken out of geographical context, and included Mud Lake and Wal-pole Island, and the two Iroquois reserves of the Six Nations and Tyendinag (See map, p. 43.)

Mud Lake (Chemong)

In 1828, Mr. Scott of the New England Company visited the Indians on the Scugog and Mud Lakes, and found them "desirous of civilization". He immediately opened a school at Mud Lake (NEC 1829:16), and built houses for the Indians at Rice and Mud Lakes. In 1835, he hired a couple to manage a soup kitchen and teach cultivation. In 1836, the Indians petitioned the Lieutenant Governor that the grant of 1600 acres on the Chemong Lake should be confirmed to the New England Company in trust for their benefit, which it was.

Scott's management of Chemong failed badly during these years, and he died in 1837, after a long illness. He was replaced by John Gilmour, a Baptist (NEC 1840:29-75, 80). At the beginning of 1838, there were eighty-five people in fifteen families at Chemong. Gilmour hired a farmer and schoolteacher. The Methodists from Rice Lake preached at Chemong and claimed the Indians as their people; however, Gilmour did not object. According to Peter Jones, at the split between the two Methodist confer-ences, the majority remained with the Canada Conference (CG Jan. 20, 1841:50), but the Rice Lake Indians, who were with the British Confer-ence, reported that there were only fourteen members of the Canada

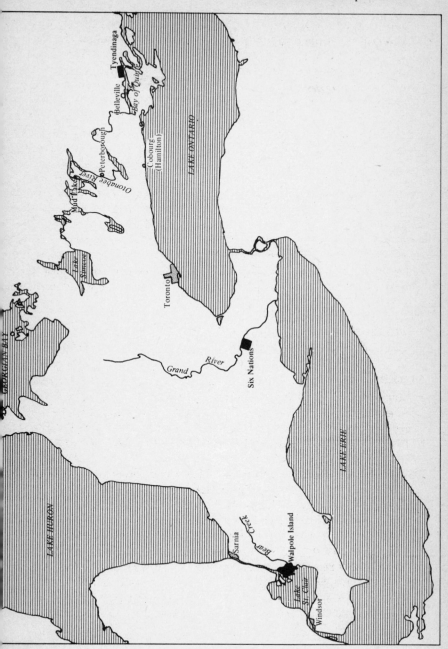

GEORGIAN BAY

LAKE HURON

Mud Lake

Lake Simcoe

Otonabee River

Peterborough

Belleville

Bay of Quinte

Tyendinaga

Cobourg
(Hamilton)

LAKE ONTARIO

Toronto

Grand River

Six Nations

LAKE ERIE

Sarnia

Bear Creek

Walpole Island

Lake St. Clair

Windsor

Conference and the rest were with the British Conference! (RG10, vol.
127, Paudash and Ibego to Jarvis, Feb. 8, 1841). This is an obvious case
of the kind of bias to be found in the reports.

With the death of the old chief, Squire Martin, in 1842, there was
competition for the chief's position. Peter Nogee became chief, but was
challenged by twenty others. Peter Nogee finally resigned in 1858, and
John Bigman was appointed chief.

By 1868, there were 160 people at Mud Lake.

Walpole Island

In 1838, J. W. Keating was appointed superintendent of the Lower St.
Clair reserve. By 1842, he had managed to expel most of the white
squatters on the island, and many of the Indians were living in squatters
houses (CR 1847:App. 21).

In May, 1841, a Church of England clergyman, James Coleman, was
appointed missionary. Coleman had no success in converting the Indians.
He attributed his failure to problems with the interpreter; however, Keating commented that Coleman's personality was unsuitable; he was too
timid and embarrassed (CR 1847:App. 21). In 1843, Coleman was replaced by John Carey who had been a missionary at Muncey, but he spent
a lot of time with the white settlers, and in 1844 he quarrelled with Keating and left the island. Towards the end of April, 1844, two Jesuit priests
came to Walpole Island to establish a mission. They were told by Keating
that because of the law excluding whites from settling on the island they
would have to obtain permission from the Governor, but in the meantime
they could camp on the island. They set up their tent and a temporary
chapel, and began to visit the Indians in their houses. On the first Sunday,
an Indian told them that during the night a messenger of the agent had
gone to all the houses to order the Indians not to attend the Catholic
service, but to go to the English service. In a council convened by Keating on April 29, 1844, the chief said they did not want the Christian
religion, but one of the Jesuits opened a school (SJ, Du Ranquet, April 30,
1844). Finally word came from the Governor that if there were Catholics
on the island, they could not be refused permission to build. The Indians
made continual efforts to persuade the priests to leave the island, but
during the winter of 1845-6 the latter reported a congregation of more
than sixty Indians, and several people had built houses near the church.

At the beginning of May, 1846, forty Catholic Potawatomi Indians came from the United States to live on Walpole Island. The enemies of the Catholics said the Jesuits had imported them, and this event was the occasion for renewed verbal attacks on the mission, with councils and petitions. In 1846 the administration of the Indian Department changed, and Clench was put in charge. He invited the Catholics to go to Manitoulin Island, and ordered the priests to leave Walpole island. The priests petitioned the Governor, who replied that the priests must submit to the wishes of the majority of Indians. The priests then claimed that the majority of the Christians on the island were Catholics, and did not leave (RG10, vols. 123, 149). On March 22, 1849, the Catholic Church and mission house were burned to the ground. The Jesuit, Du Ranquet, continued the mission from a bark hut, but his Bishop eventually decided to close the mission.

During 1845, the Church of England dismissed Carey and appointed Andrew Jamieson as missionary. On July 19, 1846, Andrew Jamieson had his first baptism of converts, two heads of families and their sons, but he still met with considerable opposition from the conjurors* (SP, Jan. 23, 1847). Jamieson remained on the island until his death in 1885, and seems to have gained the affection of the Indians. He learned the language and acted as letter writer and intermediary in business with the Government. By 1861, he had baptized 400 of the population of 750 (Pascoe 1901:173).

In 1857, the Wesleyan Methodists established a mission among the Potawatomies who had previously refused any attempts to convert them (WAR 1857:xxi). By 1860, 160 members were reported, but by 1863 there was not a permanent missionary, and in 1866, a large band of people returned to the United States. During the 1870's the mission revived. The Potawatomies lived on their own island, and the Methodist mission was quite separate from the Church of England.

Six Nations

In 1831, a quarrel between Lugger and Brant reflected differences between Methodists and the Church of England people, and the Upper and Lower Mohawks. Brant reinstated a schoolteacher who had been fired by Lugger. The Lower Mohawks, who supported Lugger and the Church of England, petitioned the Governor for a white man as agent in place of Brant, whom they accused of barring them from the council house. Brant died in 1832, and William Richardson became the agent for the New

*A class of medicine man.

England Company. By 1833, the population had increased to about 2300, and the NEC operated seven schools. Early in 1834, the Mohawk Institute was opened to boarders.

By 1836, the Methodist mission had expanded to ten regular Sabbath appointments. In 1842, some Baptists came from the United States to the Grand River to work among the Tuscaroras. One of the Church of England catechists, John Obadiah, who had quarrelled with the missionary over the right of the catechist to exhort in the church and be first to receive Holy Communion, threatened to leave the church; he was persuaded to remain, but his three friends and many of the congregation joined the Baptists (SP, Elliot, June 9, 1842). According to the Baptist reports (1842), the number baptized by total immersion in the Grand River during the revival in 1842 was eighty-eight.

In 1838, the Six Nations had 257,000 acres of their original 300,000 acres remaining (NEC 1846:125). In 1841, the Indians objected to government orders that they should be moved to the south side of the river to a tract of 20,000 acres. The Executive Council increased the size of the reserve to 55,000 acres in October, 1843, but the Indians apparently did not hear about it until the summer of 1844 (NEC 1846:150-151). The Indians experienced a great deal of insecurity during this transaction. The movement of the Indians to the south side of the river entailed considerable reorganization for both the New England Company and the Methodists, whose schools and churches were on the north side of the river. In 1848, with the union of the Canadian and British Methodists, the Canadian Methodists moved to a log chapel on the south side of the river which had been occupied by the British Methodists. Methodist attempts to expand their mission to the non-Christian nations met with considerable opposition from the Church of England missionaries. The following incident reported by Mr. Heyland, illustrates the bitter feeling between them:

> When the late Moses Walker was on what proved to be his deathbed, he sent a message by one of our Interpreters to the Rev. Mr. Heyland, requesting to see him before he died. When the messenger arrived, Mr. Heyland was from home; but on his return, learning that the above message was left for him, he without delay set out for the sick man's residence. But before he arrived at the place he was informed that the man was dead, and that nearly the last words which he uttered were, "Tell Mr. Heyland I am a member of his Church: I wish him, therefore, to attend my funeral, and to bury me according to the rites of the Wesleyan Methodist Church". Mr.

Heyland was made acquainted with this, and he therefore prepared himself to attend to the request of the dying man. The place and time of interment were appointed, and to all appearance everything was going on in accordance with the desires of the widow and family. But some of Mr. Walker's relations were determined to frustrate the wishes of the deceased, as above expressed, and those of his family. Hence they secretly made arrangements with the Rev. Messrs. Nelles and Elliott to have him buried according to the formularies of the Church of England. When the friends of Mr. Walker removed the body from his late residence to the graveyard, a distance of five or six miles, they had to pass by the house in which Divine Service is held by Mr. Nelles in order to get to the Methodist Chapel. When opposite the door of said house, they were ordered to stop. The coffin, containing the body was unceremoniously taken out of their hands and, to their great surprise and mortification was conveyed by other hands into the aforementioned place of worship and the funeral service of the Church of England was performed by Messrs. Nelles and Elliott. (WAR 1848:xii)

During the 1850's, things settled down and reports were concerned with fluctuations in the mission work, but there were no outstanding events.

Tyendinaga (Bay of Quinte)

In 1831, the Church of England appointed Saltern Givins the missionary to the Mohawks of the Bay of Quinte, and he also acted as an agent for them with the Government. Some of the Indians were Methodists, including Chief Abraham Hill, and did not agree on policies with the other chiefs, as they were planning to move to the Grand River. There were also tensions and quarrels between the hereditary chiefs and the warriors who wanted more power, and in 1847, the system of government was changed to a council of two chiefs, two councilmen and a secretary, who were appointed to manage the affairs of the nation (RG10, vol. 409, Loft et al. to Anderson, March 29, 1848). This did not stop the factionalism between the parties of Powles Claus and John Hill which had existed in the 1830's, and the disputes between them continued throughout the fifties (RG10, vols. 408, 411, 412, 420). In the 1857 census the population was 562 (CR 1858:88).

Summary

With the government schemes to civilize the Indians launched in 1830, the Indians lost their internal autonomy to the combined or competing efforts of missionaries and government agents, and with the change of government policy in 1836, they lost the optimism that had characterized government work. During the 1840's the Indians lost more of their land, and most of the remaining Indian groups came under missionary care. The gradual formation of social and physical boundaries around the reserves which were indirect effects of these policies, led to an increase in competition between Indians, missionaries and agents, for the right to make decisions about the affairs of the Indians. It has been demonstrated in this chapter that quarrels between missionaries, between missionaries and Indians, agents and missionaries. between Indians, etc., became much more frequent during the 1840's and 1850's. These quarrels hampered missionary work, and the missionaries' right to initiate changes was challenged by their competitors. During the 1850's and 1860's there was a decline in the amount of information reported by missionary and government agents as the work became more routine.

CHAPTER IV

RELIGIOUS BELIEFS AND PRACTICES

There were two explicit roles the missionaries played as ministers of religion: the missionary role of trying to change beliefs and practices, and the ministerial role of setting up a church organization. The implicit roles they played in effecting political, economic and more general social changes will be considered in later chapters.

It is extremely difficult to determine the nature and extent of changes in the belief system of a group in an historical study. Without a written statement of belief such as the Bible, there is practically no way of knowing about the religious beliefs held by the Indians before the missionaries came, and in most cases equally hard to measure the changes. Ideally, one would study the beliefs of the Indians at a former point in time, and then select another point in time, examine the new beliefs, and discuss some of the intervening processes. However, the evidence is so sparse at all stages, that any attempt to reconstruct the "aboriginal religion" as a total system is doomed to failure. In the first place, there were various groups of Iroquois, Ojibwa and Delaware, with different dialects. None of these groups was indigenous to southern Ontario, and all had moved around considerably, with much contact with other groups for many decades. The Moravian Delawares and the Mohawks were converted early in the eighteenth century, the Ojibwa and the Iroquois and Munsees had mixed a lot, and most of them had been in contact with whites for some time. It is my intention to describe the aboriginal religious systems as they appeared to the missionaries, or as they were described by Indians to the missionaries at the period of missionary work. This means relying on the accounts of Ojibwa religion given by Peter Jones and George Copway, both of whom became Methodist missionaries. Peter Jones was only half-Indian, and before his conversion to Methodism, had been living with a Mohawk family at the Grand River, rather than with his mother's kin, the Mississaugas of the Credit. Neither account, therefore, is likely to be "pure", but they are probably both fairly representative of the kinds of religious beliefs held by the Ojibwa at that time.

They seem to be agreed that there was a Good Spirit, *Gitchi Manito,* and an evil spirit, *Muhji Manito,* and innumerable other spirits (manitos) which inhabited natural objects. Both say that more sacrifices were offered to the evil spirit. Jones mentions various feasts. Copway has more to say about the Midewiwin or Medicine society. (See Appendix II, p. 98.) Religious experience for the individual Ojibwa involved both a personal and a group experience. The personal experience came throug dreams and omens, and involved a relationship between a person and certain spirits. The group experience involved the Midewiwin which required initiation and various degrees of membership according to knowledge. Mediating between the individual and manitos were several classes of shamans, some individual, and some members of the Midewiwin. Copway describes the Midewiwin society, and James Evans (a missionary) describes ceremonies which took place at St. Clair in the 1830's (see Appendix p. 101). Evans also recounts the tale of a prophet who became converted to Christianity, which illustrates the importance of the individual religious experience among the Ojibwa. It is interesting that Peter Jones comments that he never had any visions or dream experiences until he became a Methodist.

Alvin Torry and Peter Jones describe some Munsee ceremonies, but there is not very much information about their beliefs. There is very little information about the non-Christian groups on the Grand River, which is odd in view of the fact that the sect of Handsome Lake must have been making its impact on the Six Nations groups just after the turn of the century. In general, the missionaries were not interested in Indian religious practices.

Without written statements of belief from the Christian Indians, similar problems arise in assessing changes of beliefs. The Wesleyan Methodists and the Moravians wrote down some of the statements of belief given by the people during prayer meetings and love feasts, but there is little material of this kind from the Church of England missionaries. It is tempting to examine the teachings of the missionaries and their concepts of God, and to presume that this was the kind of theology that was learned. However, this approach begs the question and invalidates any comparative study of the extent to which certain kinds of Christian theology and religious beliefs were compatible with Indian beliefs.

The Methodists

The Methodists recorded many of the testimonies and confessions of faith spoken by the Indians at prayer meetings and love feasts: for example, here are some of the remarks recorded at a love feast with the Rice Lake Indians in 1827:

> *Pottosh* — "Brothers and sisters, I will tell you what the Great Good Spirit has done for me. Not long since, I was a poor wretched man. I did not know good. But I have lately found it, and it makes me very happy. I will always bow down to the Lord as long as I live."

> *A woman* — "My happiness is so great, since I found the Great Good Spirit, that it seems to me as if it was but one day."

> *A man* — "O thank God that he has washed my heart from sin. I desire to go to heaven, to see my Saviour and all the good people that's gone above."

> *A woman* — "The Great Good Spirit has cast away all my sins from me. I now feel very happy in looking to him. I love to hear the black coats, tell us about Jesus and the good way."

> *A woman* — "The Great Good Spirit fills my heart with love. I hope to go to heaven. I have seen that happy place. I pray for all that they may go to heaven. I thank the ministers for the good they give us. I hope we may all escape the fiery place of hell."

> (CA & J, May 5, 1827:170)

There were also descriptions of actual conversions, both from the missionaries' and the Indians' points of view. Torry describes the first meeting with the Mohawks after the camp meeting at which Peter and Polly Jones were converted:

> The house was crowded and many gathered around the windows and doors. There were several there who had been awakened to a sense of their lost and ruined condition, by the efforts of Peter and Polly. I commenced the exercises, it was not long before sobs and cries broke from every part of the house; men and women, old and young, crying out "O, my sorry, wicked heart! O, my sorry, wicked heart! I shall go to the bad place!" The scene was solemn and impressive. Scattered all over the room, were eighteen or twenty, who were wringing their hands, and crying as though their hearts were breaking under some great grief; while others, crowding up to see what was the matter, looked on in wonder and awe. . . . We said to them, "Jesus Christ, the son of the Great Spirit, and who lives with the Great Spirit above, will save you. He will cast the bad spirit out of your hearts, and make your sorry, wicked hearts good and glad, like Polly's and Peter's. If you will say in your hearts, to the Great Spirit, and his son

Jesus Christ, that you will put away the fire-water, the white
man's poison, and drink no more of it; that you will not be wicked
any more; that you will do all this Bible tells you to do . . . and
you must believe that Jesus Christ can drive the bad spirit out
of your hearts and make them glad and happy, by entering in
himself."

They seemed at once to believe these gospel truths . . . and
simultaneously with their believing, they fell from their seats
either to the floor or into the arms of some one near by, and to
all appearance were dead persons. The Indians at the doors and
windows, and those in the house, were very much frightened
at this, and ran for water . . . but before water could be brought
. . . they had begun to drink of the waters of salvation. In a few
moments the shout of victory was heard from those who, a few
moments before, seemed plunged in hopeless despair . . . their
tongues were loosed, and from all parts of the house was heard
the cry, "O Jesus, he make me happy! O Jesus, how I love thee!
Glory! Glory!"   (Torry 1864:79-81)

It seems likely that the kinds of beliefs and emotions involved in this
experience were not very different from those found in Indian religious
systems. George Copway, an Ojibwa from Rice Lake, described his own
conversion which occurred at a camp meeting near Colborne in 1830:

In the evening, one of the white preachers . . . spoke; his text was,
"for the great day of His wrath is come, and who shall be able
to stand." . . . He spoke of the plain and good road to heaven;
of the characters that were walking in it; he then spoke of the bad
place, the judgement, and the coming of a Saviour. I now began
to feel as if I should die, *I felt very sick in my heart.* Never had
I felt so before; I was deeply distressed, and knew not the cause.
I resolved to go and prostrate myself at the mourners bench, as
soon as an opportunity offered. We were now invited to approach.
I went to the bench and knelt down by the roots of a large tree.
But how could I pray? I did not understand how to pray; and
besides, I thought that the Great Spirit was *too great* to listen
to the words of a poor Indian boy. What added to my misery
was, that it had rained in torrents about three quarters of an hour
and I was soaking wet. The thunder was appalling, and the light-
ning terrific. I then tried again to pray, but I was not able. I did
not know what words to use. My father then prayed with and
for me. Many were praising God, all around me. The storm now
ceased, and nearly all the lights had been extinguished by the rain.
I still groaned and agonized over my sins. I was so agitated and
alarmed that I knew not which way to turn in order to get relief.
I was like a wounded bird, fluttering for its life. Presently and

suddenly, I saw in my mind, something approaching; it was like
a small but brilliant torch; it appeared to pass through the
leaves of the trees. My poor body became so enfeebled that I fell;
my heart trembled. The small brilliant light came near to me, and
fell upon my head, and then ran all over and through me, just as
if water had been copiously poured out upon me. I knew not how
long I had lain after my fall; but when I recovered, my head was
in a puddle of water, in a small ditch. I arose; and O! how happy
I was! I felt light as a feather. I clapped my hands and exclaimed
in English, *"Glory to Jesus."* (Copway 1847:83-85)

This kind of experience seems to have been very common. John Simpson,
the principal chief of the Grape Island Indians, testified at a love feast:

Before I got religion I was very wicked. Brother Sunday took
great deal of pains, told me about Jesus. I feel very bad; did not
know what to do with myself; my head began to be very bad;
I could not sit up; I did not know myself what the matter was;
I did not know how very bad my heart was; I sat down little,
walked a little, rolled about little; did not know what to do. Brother Sunday then prayed to the Great Spirit for me. I feel some
good in my heart. I compel to cry. I went to camp meeting,
I still did not know what to do. I heard of a God in heaven. I
did not before think anything about it. I then prayed God bless
me a poor Indian. I was great while in great trouble in my heart.
Before camp meeting went away, my heart jump very high. Jesus
bless me all over, soul and body too. Since my heart changed, I
love every body. . . . (CA & J, Oct. 17, 1828:26)

Apart from these confessions and testimonies from love-feasts as to the
acceptance of Christianity, in the form of an emotional experience,
in which Jesus saved them from their sins and made them happy, there
are many instances of the formal renunciation of Indian practices; for
example, the conversion of a Chippewa man from the Thames region,
who immediately gave the missionary his medicine bundle (CA & J,
Jan. 4, 1828:70). Sault, a former conjuror at St. Clair, described how
he "bade farewell to my master, the Devil and broke his whiskey bottle
as a token" (MMN, Stinson, Dec. 15, 1840), and there are many other
cases. The settlement of "Spook Island" in Rice Lake is an example of
the formal renunciation of beliefs. This island was named from the belief that spirits had been seen near the graves of the dead, and many
people were afraid of being found alone near the place. Since the conversion of the Indians, the dead had not been known to disturb the
living with their appearance, and, according to Case, the "converts have

no longer any apprehensions, either from Mah-che-nun-e-too, that is
the Evil Spirit, nor from the ghosts which they once apprehended walked
among the graves of the dead" (CA & J, Sept. 19, 1828:10).

The process of organizing the church consisted of receiving the
Indians into the society by baptism, then forming various classes of
instruction, with class leaders. When the Mississaugas of Belleville were
baptized and formed into a society in 1826, they were placed under the
care of two of their principal men, Capt. William Beaver and John Sunday, who acted as leaders (MM 1826:310). When the Credit Indians
settled at the Credit, and a church was built, Case and Peter Jones
divided them into classes and selected two of the "most intelligent and
experienced men" to take charge of each of the classes. The classes met
once a week. The class-leaders in turn met with the missionary every week,
at which time the missionary enquired into the state of the classes and
gave the leaders advice (Torry 1864:187). Peter Jones looked after the
formation and regulation of classes on his tours around the country.

The following description illustrates the process of baptism and the
means by which people were admitted into society:

> On Monday afternoon we proceeded to an examination of the
> assembly in regard to the Christian experience. And the result
> was, that the whole body of about sixty adults had become re-
> formed in their manners so as to give up the use of spirits, and
> all but about ten professed to have received the hopes and
> joys of the gospel. The converted natives we invited forward
> for baptism, while those who had more recently been awakened,
> were told that, when they should be able to declare the mercy
> of God to their souls, they also would hereafter be admitted to
> the ordinance, and they were requested to retire to the rear of
> the congregation. When they arose to retire, they began to weep,
> and then to pray that the Great Good Spirit would now have
> mercy on them. When we perceived how deeply they were
> affected, we sent some of the most experienced Indian brethren
> to engage in prayer in their behalf. During the exercise of prayer
> the Spirit of Grace appeared to be powerful on the minds of the
> penitents. And in the course of about an hour, nine persons pro-
> fessed to have found peace to their souls.
>
> The most of those present had been reformed from their drun-
> ken habits for several months, and now having become so deeply
> impressed with a sense of their sins and of the blessings of their
> Saviour, we concluded to admit all the converts with their families
> to the ordinance of baptism.
>
> The nature and design of the ordinance were now ex-
> plained, and we proceeded to propose the formulary,—

"Dost thou renounce the devil with all his works?" Again we paused to give them further instruction in regard to the extent of Satan's power and influence. For the natives of the Chippeway had been terribly afraid of the evil spirit (Muchemuneto) and to avert his displeasure, have made their offerings and paid their devotions generally to him.

We informed them from the Scriptures, that Satan had no power, but to tempt to evil, and to punish the wicked. . . . While on this subject they appeared unusually moved, and when we again proposed, "Dost thou renounce the devil with all his works?", they responded with great earnestness and with a strong voice, 'Aah'! and some of them put down their feet, as if treading the power of Satan beneath them. Seventy-five now received baptism, about sixty of whom were over the age of ten years. On the same evening, the Lord's Supper was administered to the adults who had been baptized. (MM 1827:228)

Many Indians were trained as native exhorters and preachers, and some as ministers. Peter Jones, though only half-Indian, was considered an Indian by the Methodist Church, and he was the first to be appointed a missionary. Others followed as missionaries, including George Copway, Peter Jacobs, William Herkimer, and John Sunday and Charles Halfmoon. It was certainly the aim of the Methodists in the early days to train Indians to fill these positions.

The Church of England

During the early years of the work in Upper Canada, the Church of England was concerned with maintenance of the church among the Indians already converted, rather than with proselytization. The Mohawks of Tyendinaga and the Grand River had been converted before their move to Canada, and baptism of new members of the church was generally confined to the children who had been born since the missionary's last visit.

There is little information about beliefs at any period. The missionaries seem to have presented a more scholarly approach than the Methodists. Great reliance was placed on the liturgy and on the aesthetic aspect of the services — there are several mentions of the singing, and how the Indians liked to sing. The missionaries would visit the people in their houses and talk to them, and great emphasis was placed on the importance of the schools.

The church organization was fairly simple. The missionary appointed a catechist to assist him. In the early days at the Bay of Quinte and the

Grand River, most of the services were taken by the catechists, and
the missionary only visited the communities twice a year or so. Participation for the majority in the church was a question of participation in the
services, which would mean attending and joining in the singing and
responses, with very little opportunity for individual expression. At
Muncey, however, Richard Flood, in 1837, had Halfmoon, Snake and
Hoff as interpreter and exhorters. Andrew Jamieson on Walpole Island
in 1869, had ten picked men as an acting committee (but it is not clear
whether these formed a church or a general council). Similarly, Edmund
Wilson at Kettle Point in 1869, picked an Indian Committee of four
men who were to interview boys who wanted more education. So there
were positions within the church for certain people.

The Church of England missionaries placed importance on the training of Indian catechists. Wilson set up a school for catechists at Sarnia
(but did not stay there more than two years), and catechists ran the
missions at Muncey, Saugeen, Kettle Point, Sarnia, and other places. The
catechists could cause trouble for the missionary if they felt they did
not have enough power, as at Tuscarora in the 1840's. The catechist level
seems to have been as far as Indians got in the hierarchy in this area, none
becoming ordained as missionaries (Henry Chase is a possible exception).

The Moravians

The roles the missionaries played as ministers of religion in the Moravian
community became almost entirely confined to the part they played in
an organized church, as opposed to their strictly missionary role. The
Moravian Indians had been converted to Christianity many years previously, and it was the Christian Indians who had come with the missionaries to Canada, so presumably the Indians who joined the missionaries
had a firm commitment to Christianity. However, it should not be forgotten that the missionaries represented a measure of security in a world
that had been very troubled during the wars in the United States, a factor creating a strong tie.

The beliefs of the Indians followed the Moravian church beliefs in an
emotional love for the Saviour, and a deep consciousness of sin. One
woman confessed:

> Although I led an outwardly righteous life, when I was yet
> among the heathen, and in consequence looked upon myself as
> better than many others, even among the believers, yet since
> my mind has been enlightened by the spirit of God, I behold

vations can be made about the kinds of beliefs that were retained, and some logical possibilities in the kinds of change that might have occurred can be suggested.

Although only a relatively small proportion of each community were active members of the church at any time, the decline in indigenous religious practices probably had an eroding effect upon the Indian belief systems. Some comments from missionaries and Indians illustrate the decline in native practices, which was not necessarily a direct result of missionary intervention, but was occurring anyway:

1827, Case to Emory:

> The natives say, they have always lived in the ways of their forefathers, except that in late years, since the introduction of the firewater . . . they have very much relaxed in their ancient ceremonies . . . in the decline of their religious rites, however, the Chippeways have kept up their superstitious observances with great care. . . .   (CA & J, April 14, 1827:126)

In 1830, at Munceytown, George Turkey was asked how the Munsees were getting along in religion, and told Peter Jones:

> Some Munceys he not like it — he say he want worship old way. But I tell him, lost old way. — Old way was good. But now Munceys get their way from all nations, some from the white people, some from the Chippewas and some from other nations. Now he think he got the old way, but this is a new way, because he lost the old way. . . .   (CG 1830:300)

Beaven (1846:75) reported in 1846: "The Muncey Indians no longer hold religious ceremonies though only a small proportion are Christians," and Flood also referred to the Munsees: "they have . . . with few exceptions long since cast their idols to the moles and bats" (CEG 1854:10). In 1859, on Walpole Island, when five old people attempted to join the annual Pagan Holiday Dance, they were laughed at by the spectators. Wilson writes of Kettle Point and Sarnia:

> Pagan practices had fallen altogether into disuse. There were some Indians living who had been "medicine men", but we never heard that they practised their charms. Still there were several families who held aloof from Christianity. When spoken to about being baptized, their reply was that they thought the Christian Indians behaved worse than the Pagan Indians, and that they were afraid if they were baptized they would become as bad.
> (Wilson 1886:55)

One way of examining the question of changes in religious beliefs is to look at the similarity or "fit" between the two systems. If there is a close fit, then large changes are not necessary, though they may in fact appear to be considerable. The fit between the Indian religions and the Christian religions was not particularly close. The Indians had a large number of spirits in their system which did not fit with the Protestant systems. However, the possibility of merging the God and the Devil of Christianity with Gitchi Manito and Muhji Manito was clear to both Indians and missionaries (as was evident in the passage on baptism among the Methodists, p. 54). In fact, the similarity between the belief systems in this respect was often used as a reason by the Indians for rejecting Christianity; they had a similar but different religion of their own, and if God had wanted them to be Christians he would have sent them the Bible and Christ (and the Indians would not have treated Christ so badly). There is some similarity between the Methodist experience of conversion through the Holy Spirit, and the vision experience of the Ojibwa.

Not all the ritual was incompatible. The agricultural festivals of the Iroquois and Delaware perhaps have their counterparts in the harvest festival and rogation ceremonies in the Church of England. The Mohawks used their condolence ceremony to sympathize with their missionary on his bereavement, and said they came as Christian people, but could still condole as previously. However, the hunting and gathering economy of the Ojibwa did not fit with the pastoral idiom of the Bible.

There is a lot of evidence that beliefs in sorcery, witchcraft, and the effectiveness of magical practices in curing, did not disappear or change. Cases in which the missionaries reported the belief in witchcraft or use of sorcery (usually referred to explanations or cures of illnesses.) Some examples include many reports from the Moravian missionaries. Zeisberger wrote in 1796:

> At a service in the evening we discoursed about sicknesses and how the savages deal with them, it being reported that such a one was bewitched, and a doctor must come and cure him; that the doctors however, were liars and deceivers, but that they believed in the Saviour, and should hold all such things folly, and have no faith in them. . . . Br. Zeisberger told them that he had no fear of Indian witchcraft hurting him, and still he was only a man like themselves; he granted that if they believed in it, it could hurt them, but they had only themselves to blame if they believed in lies and not in the Saviour. . . . We have always found it needful to be on our guard that Indian superstition shall not crop out and be again established when we have peace from without.
> (Bliss 1885 II:456)

In 1798, Zeisberger fired all the assistants, one of the reasons being that some had had "witchcraft used over them by Indian doctors" (Bliss, 1885, II:505). An account from 1831 shows the problem was still with the missionaries:

> The funeral of three children . . . took place. The parents of the latter having successfully buried three children out of four, suffered themselves to be influenced by their heathen relations who ascribed the deaths which occurred among the Christian Indians more frequently than in the Muncey town to the prevalence of sorcery. What added to their suspicions was the circumstance that the mother of the deceased child had at different times heard the crowing of a cock at night before her door, which was interpreted as a hostile noctural visit on the part of some evil disposed person, having the faculty of assuming the shape of an animal in order to inflict death by poison. (MI 1831: 428)

In the *Missionary Intelligencer,* which covers the period after 1822 quite thoroughly until about 1835, there are at least a dozen mentions of sorcery, but there is only one instance in all the deaths where there is mention of someone dying immune to Christianity because he believed he had been bewitched (MI 1833:425). It appears that there was an intellectual acceptance of Christianity and rejection of witchcraft, but an emotional residue of belief in witchcraft which the Indians resorted to in difficult times or when a case arose that seemed to defy logical explanation.

Wilson (1886:55) at Sarnia, mentioned that the Indians remained very superstitious even after their conversion to Christianity. "They never seemed to lose altogether their faith in witchcraft, especially in that form by which it was believed that certain persons had power to cause sickness or misfortune to others."

It seems that sickness was one of the areas where the benefits of Christianity were not so noticeable. In those days, healing was still largely a matter of faith, rather than medicine. However, even science cannot explain certain things about sickness, e.g., why particular people are victims. Christianity is also somewhat inadequate on this question. How can it be God's will that people should suffer, if God is good? Witchcraft beliefs can present more satisfactory answers to these questions, and it is not unreasonable that people should hang on to them. Perhaps it is more difficult to renounce beliefs that are based on fear.

CHAPTER V

POLITICS AND ECONOMICS

In this chapter the roles played by missionaries in political and economic change are considered. Being outside the strictly "religious" sphere, these roles may be expected to overlap sometimes with those claimed by agents of the Government. There is some evidence of this structural conflict. By corollary, interaction with rival missions and with the Indians themselves begins to be seen as competition for political influence and economic resources. It is important to notice, however, that not all these effects were intended by the protagonists; nor was the effort to "civilize" and so Europeanize Indian groups seen by either side as a denigration of Indian culture.

Politicians and Administrators

Political processes involve the determination and implementation of public goals, and the differential distribution and use of power (Swartz 1968:1). Therefore, the power to make decisions and implement them is crucial to the political process, and in order for the missionary to play a political role in the community, he had to have power of this sort. The source of the political power of the missionary was an important variable in determining the kind of political role played by the missionary in the community. There were various sources of power or legitimacy that were significant for missionaries in southern Ontario, including the ownership of land, or the right to use land, the backing of the colonial Government, the demand for the services offered by the missionary, and the permission or request of the chief for the services of a missionary. The Moravians relied almost entirely on their occupation of the land for legitimacy, and when this was challenged by the Indians, they lost their power in the community. A similar fate occurred to the New England Company at Mud Lake.

The backing of the colonial Government was used by the Church of England missionaries to establish their legitimacy and discredit their rivals, and the Indians were often anxious to belong to the established church. The Methodists, on the other hand, had to go to some lengths to prove that they were not opposed to the Government, and also had the backing of the Government: e.g., Torry, in his first visit to Muncey-town: "I now informed them that I was a Methodist minister, and was patronized by the Governor and their agent. . . . " (1864:116).

The request of the Indians and their chief for a missionary was frequently very important for the legitimacy of the missionary. Where the chief was against the missionaries, as in the case of the Roman Catholics at Walpole Island, they did not get anywhere in establishing a mission. However, where the missionary managed to become a chief (Peter Jones at the Credit), he was able to secure a position of great influence on the council. No matter how legitimate the missionary's position, however, did the missionaries actually play important roles in decision making and implementation in the communities?

In southern Ontario, very few missionaries had any formal political role to play in the official administration. At Moraviantown, the missionaries originally drew up the rules and ran the administration of the community. If people did not like the rules or keep them, they were asked to leave. Peter Jones was a member of the council at the Credit (appointed unanimously in 1829) and drew up the rules for the community in 1830, but his case is a bit different since he played the role of an Indian, as well as that of missionary. At Grape Island, the missionaries also drew up rules for the community; the community being one established by the missionaries for the Indians, rather than vice versa (CG, Feb. 13, 1830: 99). These sets of rules can be found in Appendix III, p. 105.

In general, the missionaries did not attend councils unless invited, let alone sit on them or preside over them. Some groups made use of the missionary as a transcriber or to write petitions. For instance, at Walpole Island, the Church of England missionary wrote down and edited the speeches for the Indians, and in 1869, he describes a change in role to only a spectator and witness in the council, because the Indians could do their own writing (SPG 1869:2). However, a New England Company report mentions that, "Mr. Jamieson has succeeded in persuading the Indians to elect a certain proportion of the members of the governing council of the Island, and he, as the representative of the Indian Department, nominates other members to sit on that council" (NEC 1871:227+n). Many of the letters to the Government found in Record Group 10 were written for the Indians by the missionary.

The power of the missionaries in most communities was limited to their influence, but this could be quite considerable. It varied from implicit influence to explicit influence such as Wilson exerted at Kettle Point: he mentions that he had to gain sufficient influence over the Indians so as to gain a majority in his favour in their council, so the CMS could establish a school (CMS, Jan. 5, 1869).

Some of the influence the missionaries acquired was through the role of mediator between the Indians and the Government. Peter Jones was active in this role. At the Credit in 1826, he discovered a discrepancy between the land payments agreed on and the amount actually received by the Indians — £50; he asked Colonel Givins for an explanation but did not receive it (Jones 1860:71). Jones was asked by the Grape Island Indians to help them petition for more land. However, when they went to York, the Governor told them (via John Strachan) that he was not willing to help them so long as they were Methodists, so this role was not always a successful one (Jones 1860:107). Peter Jones spent quite a lot of time discussing the affairs of the Indians with the Indian agents, Givins and Anderson. Conrad Van Dusen took the part of the Indians at Newash and Saugeen, and was active in representing their affairs to the Government, though without much success.

There are a couple of cases where the missionary acted as the Indian agent. Saltern Givins was the agent at Tyendinaga for a while, and Jamieson acted as representative of the Indian Department at Walpole Island.

More usually, negotiations between missionary and Government were concerned with the status of the mission, rather than the rights of the Indians.

Farmers

It was important to the missionaries to teach the Indians to farm the land, as they could not hope to keep their congregations together unless they could provide them with some alternative means of subsistence to hunting and gathering. The Six Nations and Delaware Indians already did some planting of corn, beans, squash, etc., but the Mississaugas and the other Ojibwa groups relied almost entirely on hunting and gathering. In southern Ontario, there was another pressing reason for the Indians to learn to cultivate the land, and that was the disappearance of their hunting grounds as white settlement took over more and more of the country.

Among the Methodists, much of Peter Jones' early work consisted not only of preaching to the Indians, but showing them how to clear the land, hold a plough, and plant crops. When the Mississaugas of the Credit were at the Grand River, the Mohawks lent them some land, and Peter Jones showed the Indians how to clear the land and hold a plough. There are accounts of his helping the Indians at Rice Lake to clear the land, plough, and plant corn and potatoes; advising the Scugog Indians to plant, and promising them seed potatoes to get a start; and of laying out garden plots at Grape Island and showing the men how to make gardens and plant seeds.

At all the Methodist mission stations in the 1820's and 1830's there was an emphasis on cultivation. The missionaries helped by demonstrating to the Indians, by providing them with farm implements and seeds, by working in the fields with them, and by preaching the necessity of cultivation. The manual labour schools at Alderville and Muncey were intended to teach the children farming, and model farms were attached to the schools.

The missionaries of the New England Company were particularly interested in promoting agriculture, and one of their first concerns was the provision of seeds and tools for the Indians at Lake Scugog, Rice Lake, Mud Lake, and the Grand River. However, they also wanted to teach farming methodically at Mud Lake and the Six Nations through farms attached to the schools; these farms would ideally support the schools and show the Indians how to farm. So they grew corn, wheat, potatoes, peas, beans, etc., and kept horses, cattle, pigs, and sheep.

Farming was of great importance to the Moravian missionaries, both for their own subsistence, and for the Indians. One of the first things Zeisberger did was to make sure that fields were cleared, laid out and cultivated. In the early years of the mission at Fairfield, they had quite a varied crop — turnips, corn, hay, wheat, potatoes, and pumpkins. Wheat was a new introduction, and Zeisberger mentions that the Indians were quite successful in growing it, though they preferred corn as a staple (Bliss 1885 II:455). Some of the fields were held in common, and the Indians would contribute corn for the poor, the old, the church, and needy people, when the occasion arose.

Zeisberger did not object to the Indians hunting and gathering as some of the other missionaries did; however, Zeisberger was missionary at a time when there were no other sources of meat. They hunted deer and bear, and it was not necessary for them to leave the community all winter to get meat as they did not have to go so far in those days for game. The women collected blueberries, cranberries, chestnuts, and both men and women fished in the river and made maple sugar.

In the following decades, the pattern of farming at Moraviantown did not change much, with some communal work and some individual work. They began to keep livestock, as well as cultivating, and in 1823, they had thirty-one sheep from which they got eighty pounds of wool. In 1828, they started to use draught oxen for hauling wood, and had fourteen pair of oxen to do the work formerly done by the women. By 1833 (PA, vol. 13:47), they had eighteen yoke of oxen, 140 head of horned cattle, 140 horses, and as many swine and sheep. The missionaries did not insist that they give up all hunting and gathering, but rather, seemed to welcome this diversification of subsistence. Crop failures were frequent enough, due to difficult weather conditions, that the other forms of subsistence were often necessary. Whenever there was an important communal occasion such as planting or harvesting, or a church festival, the men would go out hunting to get enough food to feed everyone while the work was being done.

With the first introduction of the gospel, the desire to clear off the land and cultivate, to demonstrate their adherence to Christianity, was very keen amongst the Methodist Indians. Later on, however, it seems that the first wave of enthusiasm wore off, and, although methods of agriculture and the principle of relying on cultivation seems to have taken hold, the rate of improvement was never quite commensurate with the initial fervour. Some reserves were not suitable for expansion. Grape Island was too small for extensive farming. The cattle had to be kept on another island two miles away, and the women had to paddle in their canoes twice a day to do the milking, which was exhausting and inefficient. This was one of the major reasons for the move to Alnwick. Snake Island, where some of the Lake Simcoe Indians finally settled, was also too small for extensive farming operations. Insecurity of land tenure was another factor preventing improvement. In many places the Indians felt that if they improved the land too much the whites would want it and they would be forced out.

Although the reports throughout the 1850's and 1860's generally describe the improvement in agriculture, there were complaints throughout the period that the Indians were away from home too much and neglected their farms. Complaints came from places as varied as Saugeen, Alnwick, and St. Clair. The test of success of the missionaries' attempts to change the means of subsistence of the Indians would be the Indians' ability to support themselves by farming. A report from Muncey in 1845 describes the Indians as self-sufficient in grain and having a surplus, but reports from Alnwick in 1857 that the women supported themselves by basket-making as they had thirty years before, and from Rama that the Indians made frequent visits to the white settlements to earn provisions (1835), are discouraging. The commissioner's report of 1858 gives a survey of conditions, which is roughly as follows: The Munsees had too little land to farm well; the Moravians had very rich land, but were torn by factions and not farming well; at Sarnia the progress was unsatisfactory — not one in twenty had raised sufficient food for the support of his family, although the land was of the best quality — recently the land had been surveyed into farm lots of about forty acres each and many of the young men who supported themselves working for the whites were clearing farms for themselves; the Saugeen reserve had rich land, but, although they had many supplies of implements, cattle and grain in 1857, they had to be partly supported by the Indian Department during the winter, and they employed a white man to plough their gardens; the Newash Indians were to go to Cape Croker where there was good land, but very little farming had been done previously; at Rama they were not doing much farming, but a lot of hunting and basket making; on Snake Island they did a lot of hunting and fishing; at Lake Scugog they were not self-sufficient, but they did not get any money for the improvements on the farms they sold. More encouraging were the reports from Alnwick, where the soil was not good, but it was tolerably well farmed; similarly at Beausoleil Island, farming was not bad, though the location was not good; many of the Mohawks of the Bay of Quinte were farming on a considerable scale; the Walpole Island Indians were putting more of their income into buying grain and farming implements than any other group; many of the Oneidas were producing a surplus; the New Credit Indians were getting their main support from their farms with some fishing — they had individual farms and farmed like white people; the Six Nations Indians also farmed like whites, and some produced a considerable surplus, and they had more or less given up hunting (CR 1858:36-93).

A description of the Sarnia Indians as good farmers, living very much like their white neighbours indicates that the division of the reserve into lots must have assisted the Indians in their farming practices to begin with (CG, Feb. 5, 1862:24). Jamieson, at Walpole Island, also describes the Indians in 1862 as having a positive attitude toward farming. They had good soil, and by 1870 they had an agricultural society with an annual show. A ploughing match at the Six Nations reserve in 1869 indicates that they must have had an agricultural society. The report from Mud Lake where the New England Company had worked with teaching farming says the Indians were still not self-supporting by 1870, though the missionaries were still giving premiums for hard work.

Although the missionaries may not have been entirely successful in changing the Indians into farmers, they did achieve a considerable measure of success, either directly by instruction, or indirectly through example and encouragement. The plants that were grown were varied; corn, beans, squash, etc., were not new to the Indians. Even if the Ojibwa had not grown much themselves, they used to buy corn from the Munsees and Iroquois occasionally. Wheat, oats, peas, and an assortment of other vegetables and fruit were new. The animals, cattle, sheep and pigs, were all new, and the implements such as the plough, and the use of oxen, were new concepts. Cultural change was therefore considerable.

Artisans and Economists

The missionaries played an important part in the introduction of European technology and industrial skills to the Indians. The missionaries were not actually artisans themselves, but in many communities they hired people to teach the Indians certain skills. For example, at Grape Island a very important establishment of the Methodist mission was the mechanics shop, and there the Indians were taught to make furniture, sleighs and shoes. It was Case's plan to defray the expenses of the establishment by selling the Indians' work, so they could afford good mechanics and lumber for cabinet-making. A similar mechanics shop was built at the Credit. The manual labour school at Alderville taught industrial skills when the Grape Island community moved. Both men and women were encouraged in "cottage industry" by the Methodists. At Grape Island, Case gave rewards to the most productive people in the production of axe-handles, scoop shovels, ladles, trays, broom handles and brooms, and the women were encouraged to make baskets, brooms, etc. The women were taught knitting and sewing, usually by the missionary's wife and sometimes by the schoolteacher, this being one of the first things taught at many of the missions. At the Credit, the women were learning to make shoes, and making quite a nice income from the sale of moccasins, in 1829.

Industry on a large scale was not attempted. In the 1830's, the Credit Indians had a good lumbering business going, with two sawmills in which they could produce 5,000 board feet every twenty-four hours. The lumber was sold in York and Niagara. It was not, however, the ideal of the Methodists to set up industries, but merely to teach the Indians useful skills, and the "arts of civilization". These skills also involved material goods, such as houses, furniture and clothes. The Indians were given instruction in how to build houses, and at Grape Island, in 1828, the missionary remarked that the Indians could build a decent house, and only needed a mechanic's help for the sash (CA & J, Jan. 9, 1829:74). At that time, they had already built twenty-six buildings, including a hospital. At the Credit, the original village was built for the Indians by the Government, but they added buildings themselves. The missionaries tried to get the people to live in houses, rather than wigwams, and furnish them with European-style furniture.

Similarly, European dress was the mark of civilization and Christianization, and was adopted by the Indians with Christianity. They were aided by the sewing and knitting classes held at the missions, and also by presents of clothes from the missionary society. A letter from Peter Jones at the Credit, in 1836, shows the changes effected by the missionaries:

> . . . They are now occupying about forty comfortable houses. . . .
> Their furniture consists of tables, chairs, bedsteads, straw-mattresses,
> a few feather beds, window curtains, boxes and trunks for their
> wearing apparel, small shelves fastened against the wall for their
> books, closets for their cooking utensils, cupboards for their plates,
> cups, saucers, knives and forks. Some have clocks and watches. They
> have no carpets, but a few have mats laid on their floors.
> . . . The clothing for the men consists of a frock coat made of
> English cloth or blanket with a scarlet belt tied around the waist.
> Calico shirts, waist coats, pantaloons, boots and shoes (but in winter
> they generally wear moccasins made of dressed deer skins) socks,
> hats, etc. . . .
> The females wear short gowns, mantles of cloth or blanket
> thrown over their shoulders, cloth petticoats, leggins, shoes or
> moccasins, stockings, broad-brimmed round hats, but many go with-
> out anything on their heads. Their hair hangs behind tied with a
> ribband, just at the back of their necks. The more civilized part
> of the women wear cloaks instead of the blankets, and have a
> shawl round their necks and shoulders exactly like the English ladies.
> (MMN, Feb. 16, 1836)

The New England Company was also interested in training the Indians in various skills through their schools, and at the Mohawk and Mud Lake Institutes they taught carpentry, blacksmithing, waggon-making and shoe-making. The New England Company also built blacksmith's and carpenter's

shops for the Rice Lake Indians. At Mud Lake, the Company provided
materials for building houses, encouraged land improvement, draining and
clearing of swamps, improving roads, and building bridges. The missionary
at Mud Lake in the 1870's had an idea for a willow-basket factory, but the
Indians were not interested.

The Church of England missionaries also encouraged the women to learn
knitting and sewing, and at Mud Lake they made their own cloth from their
sheep in 1841.

The Church of England and the Moravian missionaries also encouraged
"civilization", or the adoption of a European life-style as far as external
possessions were concerned. A visitor to New Fairfield in 1845 (MI, vol.
9:68) commented on the log houses of the Moravian Indians, some of which
"present quite a comfortable appearance" in contrast with the bark and
cloth tents of some Potawatomies who were camped at New Fairfield. In
1859, another visitor commented that there was not a male, old or young,
who wore a blanket in church; "the females . . . are more tenacious of their
old mode of dress. Those who can afford to get fine broadcloth use it instead of a blanket. Of late shawls are becoming fashionable" (PA, vol. 13,
1859:47).

The missionaries did not have to introduce the concept of money and
trading for money. The Indians had all had dealings with the Government
in the sale of lands, or compensation for lands, and of course they had been
trading with the fur traders for decades. However, much of this trade had
consisted of barter of skins for whiskey and the acceptance of Christianity
put a stop to that. Unfortunately, although Christianity helped the Indians
in their dealings with traders, as they were not so drunk and not so likely
to be cheated, they were usually very deeply in debt. The missionary at
Mud Lake would buy the furs from the Indians and then resell them to
traders, in order to protect the Indians from direct dealings with the traders
often he had to work at a loss. The Mud Lake missionary also paid the
Indians he hired to work for him in goods, rather than money. Although
he was protecting the Indians from the wider market so that they did not
participate directly in the economy of the country, he did introduce the
idea of payment for goods and services — he made the Indians pay rent for
the land, he hired people to do work, and he gave premiums to people who
worked hard at cultivating their crops. In 1858, the Mud Lake Indians were
described as being "nearly out of debt", and the Superintendent said that
they were less encumbered with debts than any other band he had visited
(NEC 1859:24).

The Indians did enter into the economic life of the wider society to some extent, by selling goods and services. The Six Nations Indians would sell corn in the winter for food and clothes for their families. The Moravian Indians produced enough grain to sell some occasionally. They also gathered berries to sell. During harvest times, the male Indians went to work for the white farmers in the neighbourhood. The missionaries did not like this, as the Indians were exposed to liquor and often pressured into drinking away their wages, but there was nothing they could do to stop it, as they realized the Indians needed the money. The Moravian missionaries allowed traders to come to the settlement and exchange goods for cattle, skins, and corn, but they refused to let any traders live in the community, though several applied for permission at various times. The missionaries did all they could to protect the Moravian Indians in their economic dealings with white people, and they arranged to have the annual presents and annuities distributed at Moraviantown so that the Indians would not have to leave the community and get cheated out of their presents.

The Methodist missionaries played a direct role in the economic life of the communities in asking for money for support for the mission. This was occasionally given from the annuities, for a church, or for the missionary's salary; for example, at Owen Sound in 1846 the Indian community paid the missionary's salary; at Saugeen in 1844, it gave £100 for the missionary's salary. In the early days, it was a struggle for people to get money together to give in the missionary collection, but if people did not have money, they earned it. In 1827, at the Credit, everyone gave money for the chapel fund, and those who did not have any money, particularly the women, went out and made baskets, brooms, etc., to sell to the whites to make money. The idea of making money to buy something necessary was important as an innovation, and there was a case of a woman at Grape Island in 1828 who made and sold enough maple sugar to buy a cow (CA & J, Oct. 24, 1828:30).

The missionaries were singularly unsuccessful, however, in introducing the profit motive, or the idea of saving, rather than living "hand to mouth". Generally, the communities did not become self-supporting in farming and the use of the industrial skills learned was not that great. The New England Company reports from the Six Nations:

> There were in 1853 about forty adults residing on the Mission who had been brought up at the Institute; the greater number of these were married and settled on land which they cultivated, and some of the young men followed the trades which they had been taught at the Institute . . . they were too apt to yield to the influence of their own people . . . by degrees adopted the careless and improvident habits for which the Indians are proverbial, though they were generally exemplary in their behaviour. . . . (NEC 1871:84)

CHAPTER VI

EDUCATION, MORALITY AND HEALTH

The areas of education, morality and health are not completely separable from the spheres of political influence and the management of economic resources, but are more diffuse in their definition and effect. In many cases Indian leaders felt that advances in "European" education, morality and health practices would enable them to cope better with political and economic changes, and to compete on more equal terms with "Europeans" and with other Indian groups. In some instances there is evidence that the religious and non-religious roles of missionaries were held to be, or hoped to be distinct — by the Indians, if not by the missionaries. In other instances it is clear that Indians and missionaries interpret the purpose and effect of the various changes quite differently; their different positions, needs and perceptions made some amount of discrepancy inevitable. Notice too that there is nearly as much variation of interpretation *among* whites and *among* Indians as there is *between* whites and Indians on this score.

Schoolteachers

The missionaries took the role of schoolteacher very seriously, and were either responsible directly for the education of the children, or hired schoolteachers for the missions. Education was important from two points of view, the civilization and Christianization of the Indians, and as a means of establishing rapport, or a place for the missionaries in the communities. Not infrequently the Indians requested education for their children from the missionaries, but not religious instruction. For example, at Muncey the Indians did not at first wish to become Christians, but when Peter Jones asked if they were opposed to having their children taught to read and write, they replied that they were not, but on the contrary, should like them taught as the white people (Jones 1860:130). There seems to have been a general hope among the Indians that the ability to read and write English would prevent them from being cheated by white men, and enable them to compete on equal terms. Chief Shawahnahness of St. Clair said in 1833:

... although they had agreed to have their children instructed
that they might understand the weights and measures used by the
white people, and that they may be able to write and keep accounts
that the white men may not cheat them, yet that they had never
engaged and had no wish to become Christians.

(MMN, Turner, May 31, 1833)

There does not seem to have been any significant difference between
the denominations in their attitude to education, and all thought that
schools were important. John Strachan wrote:

One of the most important steps towards their conversion is that of
qualifying as soon as possible native teachers and this may be done
at the mission establishments where schools ought to be kept and
with still greater effect at the college when it comes into operation.

(SL2, Strachan to CMS, March 23, 1829)

The curriculum did not vary much in the different missions. The
basic subjects were reading and writing, and most reading instruction
was from the Bible. In many schools arithmetic, natural history and
geography were common subjects on the curriculum. Reports from the
Methodist schools usually emphasized the progress made in reading and
writing, and similarly in the Church of England schools, reading, writing
and arithmetic were the most important subjects, with geography and
history as extras.

In the Methodist schools, English was probably the common language
of instruction, though the reports are not generally specific on that point.
In the early days, some use of both languages was probably necessary, as
the children did not always understand English. At Rice Lake in 1830,
the missionary had the children repeat answers in both English and Ojibwa to be sure they understood the meaning of what they were saying,
so they were obviously teaching in English. At Grape Island, one class
was translating the testament into Ojibwa, so reading it in English. At St.
Clair in 1837, the teacher reported that the children could read and write
in both English and Ojibwa very well. Yet in the 1850's, the Oneida
Indians requested an English schoolteacher as they wanted their children
to learn English, and they got an English school in 1856 (WAR 1856:xix).
In 1858, the missionary at New Credit finding himself in the position of
having to teach school for a month, expressed his dissatisfaction with the
progress the children had made in reading and writing English with understanding, and suggested:

We want a Geography of our country, also a Spelling book with

definitions of words, a short Grammar in catechetical form, and
then burn or destroy all Indian Books and put an end to talking
Indian in school. (WMN, May 1, 1858:259)

English was also the main language of instruction in the Church of
England schools, though the missionary at Mud Lake complained in
1844, that, although they could read English quite well, the difficulty
lay in getting the children to understand what they were reading. In
1859, the rule at Mud Lake was that nothing but English was to be spok-
en in the school; this measure cannot have been very successful, as the
new schoolmaster who came in 1869, learned the Ojibwa language in
order to be able to teach the children; the missionary did not approve of
this measure. In 1843, the Mohawks of the Bay of Quinte requested a
Mohawk, as well as an English school.

The Moravian missionaries originally taught school in Delaware, but in
1806, the Indians asked to have their children taught in English. The
missionary reported:

> . . . the Indians do not send their children to school unless they are
> taught English, and the missionaries object to teach them the
> language because then they hear and understand all the profane
> and filthy conversation of the rum traders. When we spoke with
> the Indian assistants on this subject in presence of the mission-
> aries Schnall and Hagen, old Jacob said that the congregation was
> unanimously of opinion that it was not proper that the Indian
> children should receive instructions from the missionaries in the
> Indian language which they themselves spoke but imperfectly,
> but they might learn it best from their parents . . . if the parents
> hearts were right with God they would know how to watch after
> their children's education and morals, but if that was not the case
> the children would be neglected, and learn a great many bad things
> from the white people, without just understanding their language.
> If they learned English they would be able to read the word of
> God . . . . It was at length agreed that English should be taught in
> the school. . . .   (PA, Vol. 4, 1806:492)

This preference for English apparently continued — in 1823, the children
were described as making good progress in learning English, and in 1838,
the missionary noted that the children were still more inclined to learn
to spell and read English than Delaware, and some of the older boys
were able to read fluently and to write a legible hand.

The missionaries in Upper Canada did not generally rely on their
own resources for teaching the Indians, but tried to employ teachers
if they had the funds. These teachers were usually male for the male

children, and female for the female school, wherever this was possible. The Methodist aim was to instruct enough Indians to become teachers, and they were successful in producing some Indian teachers, though some of the Indians became missionaries, rather than teachers. Among the Indians who taught at various mission schools were Henry Snake, William Wilson, Allan Salt, David Wawanosh, David Sawyer, Abraham Sickles, J. Elliot, Henry Steinhauer, Benjamin Crane, and John Jones, and his son Alfred Jones. The Church of England missionaries also hired teachers for their schools, and also thought it very important to train Indians to become schoolteachers, with a fair amount of success. By 1859, at the Six Nations reserve, there were four Indian school-teachers who had been educated at the Mohawk Institute working on the reserve, and five catechists. Other Indian schoolteachers included John Green, who was appointed in 1815 at the Bay of Quinte; John Jacobs' sister at St. Clair in 1868, and at Kettle Point in 1868, the Indian catechist was keeping school; and on Walpole Island there was an Indian schoolteacher for a while, who was replaced by a white schoolteacher in 1862. The Moravian missionaries or their wives or children taught the schools at New Fairfield, and the Moravians do not seem to have considered the training of Indian schoolteachers an objective.

The biggest problem faced by the missionaries was the irregular attendance of the children. Throughout the period, the Indians at most of the mission stations were dependent on hunting for part of their subsistence, with sugar-making, fishing, and some migratory wage-labour taking the Indians away from the communities for long periods of the year. Reports from the Methodist schools were optimistic in the 1830's, but by the 1860's, there were only some places with good reports, and many of the reports were discouraged because the attendance of the children at school was so irregular. Zeisberger commented in 1796 that some of the children were so enthusiastic about school that they even cut Br. Sensemann's supply of wood for him at his sugar hut so that he would not have to take time out from teaching, and that many of the boys could write a good English hand, better than the clerks in Detroit (Bliss 1885 II:438). The Moravian missionaries had the same problems of attendance as the other missionaries. In 1843, a new schoolroom was opened, and the missionaries remarked that the heated schoolroom was very attractive to the children in the winter, and attendance was boosted. The Church of England day schools also suffered, and so at the Grand River and Mud Lake reserves, where the New England Company was paying for the schools, they set up boarding schools for the children. The boarding-schools were more successful than the day schools, and the missionary at the Grand River said they should think of the day schools as feeders for the Mohawk Institute.

The Mohawk Institute was opened in 1823 by the Rev. William Hough of the New England Company as a day school. When Nelles was hired by the New England Company, the Institute included a mechanics shop, two large rooms for teaching girls spinning and weaving, and two rooms for teaching the boys tailoring and carpentering. In 1834, ten boys and four girls were taken in as boarders, in addition to the day scholars. By 1840, the number of children had increased to forty, and it was necessary to increase the staff, with a full time couple to manage the Institute, and extra people to teach the trades. In 1842, the head of the Institute reported that there were two of the boys who were almost perfect at their trades, "John Obey as a waggon maker, and William English as a cabinet maker, and three or four of those who are being taught shoe making, and it is my intention to bring before the chiefs a plan for having such of the boys who become perfect located in a convenient place to prosecute their several trades" (NEC 1846:27).

By 1853, there were about forty adults living on the reserve who had trained at the Institute, but they were not following their trades with the success that might have been expected. In 1859, there were about sixty boarders, and in 1869, there were forty-seven male pupils and forty-two female pupils (NEC 1871:101).

The missionary at Mud Lake started a boarding school in 1842, to teach academic and non-academic subjects such as farming, blacksmith's and carpenter's trades for the boys, and spinning, knitting, sewing, weaving and household economy for the girls. The experiment was started with eight children and was successful for many years. However, a report from Henry John Lister in 1869 to the New England Company suggested that the boarding school should be given up, as none of the children lived more than two miles from the school, and in 1870, the Company resolved to give up the school. They did, however, provide two suits of clothes for twelve children who attended the day school regularly, and later decided to provide dinner to the children who attended regularly (NEC 1871:152, 162). The missionary reported that they had started to give dinner to the children who were regular in attendance and well-behaved, and that the school was filled every day; there had never been such good attendance since the school was established. The schoolmaster, in addition to teaching the school, assisted at the meetings, employed the children, worked in the teacher's field, assisted in the general farming and business of the institution, studied Indian and attended to the wants of his family (NEC 1871:189).

At Alnwick, a manual labour school was started in 1839, with the emphasis on farming for boys and household economy for girls, and the report for 1841 mentioned that the committee was so impressed by the work that they had provided for a larger number of children to be boarded under the care of the missionary and his wife. Mrs. Case reported in 1841 on the progress of the school:

> The School . . . is a Manual Labour School; entirely under the control of the Missionary. The pupils are all boarded at the Institute. The number of young men is five: — of girls eight. They are taught reading and other branches of a Common English Education, including Geography, in separate buildings, the young men . . . about 25 little boys, by an Indian teacher; . . . who was instructed in this place: — the girls with 8 or 10 little ones that are day scholars, by a lady. — the young men spend six hours a day in school; except in sowing time. During the remaining hours, they are instructed in agricultural business. The girls spend also six hours a day in school: the afternoon half of which time is devoted to needlework. — during the rest of the day they are engaged in housework. The following is the daily routine of this department.
>
> They rise during winter at 5 o'clock: and in summer at half past four, The girls proceed to milk the cows: then prepare the breakfast; attend family prayer; and hear a lecture, or exposition of a portion of the Scriptures. — The singing, and all the exercises, are in English. The girls then set the cheese, and do housework — at 9 a.m. they go into school — At noon dinner. At half past one p.m. school recommences; then as above mentioned, needlework — School closed at half past four p.m. — at five, supper, at six, milking the cows. Prayers at eight p.m., at half past, they retire to rest.
>
> A considerable quantity of cheese has been sold — about 3000 lbs. in weight. In this approaching summer, spinning will be introduced and perhaps weaving.
>
>   (MMN, to Alder, April 17-19, 1841)

By 1848 the Indians at Alnwick were supporting twelve of the twenty-four children at the school, and the rest of the children and the teachers were supported by the Wesleyan Methodist Society. Allan Salt, an Indian educated at the mission school, taught the boys; the girls were taught by Miss Cook. They learned reading, writing, arithmetic, geography, book-keeping, and English grammar; in addition, the boys learned farming and the girls learned household economy. By 1854, there were three graduates of the Institute working as teachers on Indian missions (WAR 1854:xvi).

In 1850, the Industrial school at Mt. Elgin opened at Munceytown with 13 boarders, and by 1851, there were 34 boarders and 20 day scholars. They learned reading, writing and cyphering, and geography. There were two teachers — one for the males and one for the females. Almost all the clothing the children wore had been made by people connected with the Institute. The regulations were:

> The bell rings at 5 a.m. when the children rise, wash, dress
> and are made ready for breakfast. At 5.30 they breakfast;
> after which they all assemble in the large school-room and
> unite in reading the Scriptures, singing and prayer. From 6–
> 9 a.m. the boys are employed and taught to work on the farm,
> and the girls in the house. At 9, they enter their schools. At
> 12 they dine and spend the remaining time till one in recreation.
> At one they enter school, where they are taught till 3.30,
> after which they resume their manual employment till six.
> At six, they sup and again unite in reading the Scriptures, sing-
> ing and prayer. In the winter season the boys are engaged in the
> Evening school and girls are taught needle-work until 9, when
> all retire to rest. They are never left alone, but are constantly
> under the eye of some of those engaged in this arduous work.
> (WAR 1851:xii)

The Indian Department had apparently promised to provide a grant of £15 to £20 per annum to each graduate to help him settle in his community, but the missionary reported in 1856 that they had not received the promised aid, and did not have the means to settle on land among their own people, and had been compelled to remain in the Institute which had become their home (WAR 1856:xx).

Another technique was adopted in 1852:

> Their improvement in every department has been far beyond
> our warmest expectations [attachment to studies, submission
> to rules, less wandering] .... Two of the most advanced girls
> are taken alternately, mornings and evenings, for a week into
> our own family, in order to teach them what it has been found

difficult to teach them in their own department; and as a reward for good conduct, and to teach them how to demean themselves under like circumstances, they are taken on the Saturday afternoon to tea with us. This has been found to encourage and improve them very much.

(MMN, S. Rose, April 1, 1852)

They were planning to teach the girls to spin; they had bought sheep and the boys were taught to take care of them. They were also teaching the boys how to milk, and other aspects of farming.

The Alnwick school had to be closed in 1856 when the missionary and the schoolteacher died during a typhus epidemic. However, up until that time they had been making good progress. The school was reopened in 1857 with only twenty boarders — some had gone home and not returned, and others had run away. By 1859 the missionary predicted that the school would have to be closed. The Indians were opposed to the school as the funds came out of their annuities.

In 1863, the missionary at Mt. Elgin died. The previous reports of the progress of the school were good, but the school was closed for four years. It opened again in July, 1867, and soon got up to its previous enrolment level. The missionary reported in 1869 that the work was going well and the children were content — indicated by the fact that none had absconded in the previous ten months.

Successes in education were mixed, and were dependent on the interest the Indians took in education. This in turn was governed by various factors, many economic; such as whether they liked the teacher, the state of their health, their finances, etc. The role of the missionary as schoolteacher included, in most cases, the responsibility for the innovation of the educational system on the reserve and the maintenance and support of schools, as well as the actual teaching.

Social Workers

It is obvious from the foregoing sections that membership in a Christian church and espousal of its belief system involved more than just religious changes; it included changes in the way of life of the converts. Personal and domestic changes were involved.

All the missionaries were anxious to put a stop to Indian drinking, as it was very destructive. It is apparent from the descriptions of both Indians and whites that the Indians were severely incapacitated by liquor, that they were cheated out of their presents and annuities by white men in exchange for liquor, these traders attending the annual distribution of presents (MM 1825:478). There are many accounts in the Moravian diaries of fatal accidents as a result of drunkenness — burning, drowning, catching pneumonia from exposure, etc. Torry's impression of the condition of the Ojibwa in the early 1820's is as follows:

> At this time the Chippewas were not confined to any one place, but . . . moved about from place to place, and wherever a white man had erected a huckstering shop, there would they be seen, rolling in the mud like swine. Their yells, when in their drunken frolics, were frightful, and often has my horse been frightened, when passing these haunts of vice. No one cared for these poor Indians, nor would any one give them shelter from the weather, unless to get their money or their furs from them. (Torry 1864:96)

Torry also describes the trip of the Credit Indians to the Grand River in the early 1820's:

> Before starting from their homes at the Credit, they had fixed themselves out in all their finery, and dressed in their best clothes; they intended to present quite an imposing appearance, but they were obliged to pass several whiskey shops, and at each, they thought they could stop and take "just one drink around". The consequence was that long before reaching Grand River, they had parted with all their money, and much of their jewelry, besides getting their clothes stained with dirt and filth. . . . (Torry 1864:100)

The Methodist missionaries insisted upon abstinence from liquor, and this was a very important factor in conversion to Christianity. Whenever the missionaries visited the Indians to talk about Christianity, they had to wait until the Indians sobered up. When Peter Jones went to the Credit, he found them all drunk except the chief, Captain John (Torry 1864:97). At Lake Simcoe many were intoxicated (WAR 1826:19). Copway describes how they had assembled to drink when the missionaries suddenly arrived, and they had to hide the whiskey kegs (Copway 1847:76). When Peter Jones and his party went to Walpole Island, they had to wait for everyone to sober up, and so on.

The missionaries urged the Indians not to drink. For example, at Muncey, Peter Jones told the Indians of:

> . . . the evil of their present manners; — their habits of drunkenness would lead them to ruin; — the Good Spirit was angry

with their wicked practices, and they would be much happier in this life if they gave up the use of ardent spirits. To this one of the chiefs replied: — "Whiskey comes from the white man. When we have any thing to sell, whiskey is the first thing the white man offers us." Peter's reply was, "the whites are not all good. The bad whites make you drunk with whiskey." He told them of the happiness of those Indians who had given up drink, and become good men.   (MM 1826:37–8)

The message seems to have been communicated. Case reported from Belleville in 1827 that, although the Indians had seventeen months ago been poor, lazy, filthy, made wretched and miserable by intoxication, that there was not one Indian in Belleville who drank (MM 1827: 480). In 1828, a trader complained that:

> The River Credit is celebrated for its salmon fishery, and before these Indians were enlightened with divine truths a salmon could be purchased of them for a *gill of whiskey,* but now we have to pay from two to three York shillings for a fish – the Indians never, since they became Methodists, tasting a drop of spirits.   (MM 1828:390)

The report from Lake Simcoe in 1827 was that the success of the Word had been so great that drunkenness was no longer seen in the camp (MM 1828:76). In June, 1826, Case reported that more than forty of the Mississauga Indians at Belleville had entirely given up the use of "ardent spirits . . . whereas five months ago they were all habitual drunkards to a man" (MM 1826:310). In 1827, the Rice Lake Indians were reported to have "renounced intoxication and everywhere are known to be a praying people" (CA & J, April 14, 1827:126). The Indians who had been converted saw the advantages of giving up drinking. Brother Beaver, speaking of his conversion, said:

> . . . that at Belleville he once heard it stated that the Lord had done great things for his nation; that they no more drink whiskey. He said that he thought it very good thing if they do without; but, said he, the white people tell me that whiskey was made for Indian to drink. . . .   (CA & J, Oct. 17, 1828:26)

The Moravian missionaries also insisted on total abstinence, and carried on a continual fight against white and Indian neighbours who smuggled liquor into the community. The missionary societies were all in favour of the prohibition against selling liquor to the Indians; however, even when it was forbidden, the practice did not stop. The

Moravians note that whiskey was mixed with wine, beer and cider, which were not prohibited, and given to the Indians to drink. All the missionaries also formed temperance societies in the Indian communities. Even the Church of England missionaries who were not against liquor as a matter of principle, were firmly in sympathy with the Moravians and Methodists with respect to the Indians, because of the destructive effect liquor had on them.

The Methodist missionaries were also anxious that the Indians should be married according to Christian form. When the Credit Indians went to the Grand River and were converted, Torry joined all the couples in "holy matrimony" (Torry 1864:104). Apart from ensuring that the Indians followed the Christian marriage form, the missionaries were opposed to polygyny, and insisted that converted Indians give up any additional wives. Peter Jones mentions that at Scugog he got an old Indian who had two wives to consent to leave one (Jones 1860:135). At Lake Simcoe, Jones persuaded Chief Yellowhead's brother to give up one of his wives: he was unwilling to do so, and left the decision to the second wife who said she was willing to do anything that was right in the sight of God. John Aisance had three wives, and when asked to give two of them up, he said:

> I have now embraced Christianity, and am willing to do any-
> thing you tell me. I took these women when I was blind, and
> did not know that it was wrong; for we have been taught that
> a man might have as many wives as he could support, and I
> thought I could support three very well; but now my eyes are
> open to see that it is not right to have more than one wife,
> so I will part with two, and keep only the eldest and first one I
> married, with this request, that I may have the privilege of
> supporting the children by the other women that they may not
> want. (Jones 1860:152–3)

Peter Jones' version of the sequel to this was not so happy: after some years, Aisance took up with one of the other wives, and having "fallen into sin", left the Methodists and joined the Roman Catholics; he started drinking and was drowned in 1847 when he fell out of his canoe, drunk (Jones 1860:153). The Church of England missionaries also wanted the Indians to be married according to Christian form, but assumed the newly converted and baptized Indian couples to be married at baptism.

A comment that the Mississaugas of Alnwick had six half-breeds among them at the time of conversion, but that since conversion there had been no inter-marriages with whites, and only three illegitimate babies in three years, leads to the assumption that missionary influence prevented much mixing between whites and Indians after conversion. Extra-marital sexual relations were frowned upon by the missionaries. White men were not always so scrupulous, however. Solomon Waldron described the unprincipled traders at Muncey: "One . . . made an Indian woman drunk, and then ***† in sight of our door, in presence of young and old" (CG, Mar. 29, 1837:82). The values of the missionaries were not directly concerned with the kinship system as such — though Jamieson did mention that he was called upon to make a will for an Indian leaving things to his wife, which he approved of as usually the possessions went to the dead man's kin, leaving the wife destitute.

The Methodist missionaries also concerned themselves with the status of women. Torry lectured the Mohawks:

> We endeavoured to inculcate habits of industry among them; for in their pagan state they were brought up to think it was degrading for an Indian to work. His business was to sit in the council, smoke the pipe, hunt and fish, while the women had to plant the corn, beans and potatoes, hoe and gather in the harvest, chop the wood, and in fact do all the drudgery. But we told them, "Indian man plant potatoes, corn and beans, he hoe and gather in the harvest, cut the wood, and help carry the children when travelling, while the women must stay in the house, bake the bread, cook the victuals, wash, and make the clothes. . . .   (Torry 1864:89)

Case reported of the sufferings of women in many instances . . . that women did all the work and got very little of the food, and he mentioned a case of an old woman at the mission who had gone away alone to die, whom he rescued and supported. Case described a sermon he gave to the Indians at Lake Scugog:

> . . . I discoursed for nearly two hours on several duties enjoined by the gospel — as that of forbearance and forgiveness of injuries, care of the sick, and love one to another, and withal that women should never appear stubborn, and men should lift the burden from their oppressed wives, and treat them not as slaves, but as companions and friends.
>   Our breakfast being ready, I said, Now, brothers, invite your wives and daughters, and seat them by your

†Waldron's expurgation.

side at the table. At first the men looked down and
appeared reluctant; but being urged they at length gave
the invitation, and the sisters took their seats, perhaps
for the first time beside their husbands at the table. —
There was much smiling with the women when the invitation was given, and all seemed happy and cheerful
and enjoyed the season finely. (CA & J, Feb. 12, 1830:94)

Neatness and cleanliness were also associated with Christianity. For example, William Beaver, an Indian exhorter, preaching at a camp meeting
in June, 1826, said:

I tell 'em squaws they must wash 'em blanket clean —
must cook 'em victuals clean like white women; they
must all live in peace, worship God, and love one
another . . . then . . . The Good Spirit make the ground
all smooth before you. (Torry 1864:146)

and Peter Jones commented on the improvement the Grape Island
Indians had made in cleanliness in 1828—"many of the houses were
neat and clean, and the dishes washed and placed in order, like as the
house and cupboard of a white squaw" (1860:216).

In the early period of the Moravian mission, the daily lives of the
Indians, their morality and their behaviour were of deep concern to
the missionaries. Much of the guardianship of the morals of the brethren was left to the church assistants. Between 1794 and 1798, Zeisberger's diary was full of mentions of the assistants making peace
between people, particularly husbands and wives, of attempts to curb
the bad conduct of the young people, men and women, and the custom
of "gadding about" at night. There were numerous attempts to prevent
drinking, both in the community where liquor was forbidden, and outside. People who were habitually drunk were sent away. Adultery and
prostitution were frequent sins. Use of Indian "doctoring" or medicines,
witchcraft, sorcery, were other sins. The missionaries also lectured on
the discipline of children, cleanliness, keeping the Sabbath, rumour-
mongering and telling lies.

There were various sanctions imposed by the missionaries ranging
from refusing communion to public confession in the church on repentance, and expulsion from the community. It was not, however, an
easy matter to expel people from the community, as they kept
coming back with promises of reform. On many occasions the missionaries tried to send away everyone who was not a member of the

church, but found it difficult to expel people as no one wanted to leave —
they had food and kin at Moraviantown, and it was physically dangerous
for them to go out among the "heathen" Indians.

In the other period for which there is detailed documentation in the
Moravian diaries (1822-35), the pattern does not seem to have changed
much. Sins confessed to prior to communion include anger, wife-beating,
pride, being contemptuous to parents, slothfulness, lukewarm attitude
towards religion, sorcery, disorderly conduct. These seem to be more
internal sins, but the missionaries commented on many instances of sorcery, deaths which came about from intoxication, drinking, quarrelling
among the sisters, etc. There was a frequent pattern of exclusion from the
church, repentance and readmittance, and the missionaries commented
that for all the people who were good Christians, there were always several
who behaved badly.

However, although there is such an emphasis on the failures and the
sin in the Moravian reports, they did make considerable changes in the
life style and moral values of the Indians.

Doctors

Some of the missionaries played roles as doctors. Lugger, of the New
England Company at the Six Nations, gave much medical attention to the
Indians. He got the Company to send sulphate and quinine for the
Indians, and the Mohawks thanked him for the medicines and food for
the sick. Jamieson, at Walpole Island, described himself in 1854 as a
physician, doling out medicine. His wife vaccinated twenty-two Indians
in 1849, and 280 Indians in 1859 against smallpox.

The Moravian missionaries' wives did a fair amount of treating the
sick. Some instances include Mrs. Luckenbach treating scurvy in 1822,
giving bark and camomile tea to people with bilious fever in 1823, and
giving medicines to Captain Norton's wife in 1825. However, the use of
European medicine was not always effective, and the Indians believed
that their traditional curing practices were more effective. This was a
very common area of conflict between the missionaries and the Indians.

The Methodist missionaries built hospitals at Grape Island and the
Credit for the sick and women in childbirth, but they generally played
more of a nursing, than a medical role. In fact, much of the medical
care of the Indians was given by doctors, though the missionary societies
sometimes sent for and paid the doctors. In general, the role of the
missionaries was confined to visitor to the sick.

CHAPTER VII

FACTORS OF SOCIAL CHANGE

During the first half of the nineteenth century in southern Ontario, missionaries were responsible for the settlement of several communities, the establishment of Christian churches in these and many other communities, the building and staffing of schools and workshops: they also encouraged farming and a western life-style among Indian groups. Many groups who had been hunters and gatherers moving over a fairly wide territory settled in small communities and changed their way of life to that of peasant farmers. These processes and the influence of the missionaries have been discussed in previous chapters. In this chapter some of the factors relating to conversion, innovation, and missionaries as agents of change, will be discussed.

It is assumed in this study that missionaries presented the Indians with alternative belief systems and styles of life, and that the Indians chose whether or not to accept changes. However, in order to understand the processes of social change, it cannot be assumed that the response of Indians to missionaries was necessarily a direct one, and attempts must be made to discover what alternatives the Indians had in making their choices; how they perceived the alternatives; what values they held to influence their choices; and the physical and social circumstances governing the choices. Did they have a real choice in most cases, or were they obliged to make the best of unsatisfactory alternatives? Unfortunately, in a historical study, and perhaps in any study, it is impossible to acquire all this information regarding each choice situation. The circumstances must be assessed from the evidence available and the choices that are made. The major criticism of this method is that it uses a post-hoc, circular argument, i.e., this is what they did, this is what they must have wanted, therefore this is what they chose, etc. . . . However, if the analyst is aware of the drawbacks in the method, it can be used to bring the goal a step closer. A discussion of the processes of conversion will exemplify how this method is used. It is impossible to discover what was in the mind of each individual when he made the decision to convert, but some of the social and political circumstances of the time, and some of the values held by the Indians which might have influenced choice one way or the other, can be demonstrated.

Some of the reasons for conversion given by the Ojibwa between 1822 and 1830 put into relief some of the reasons for the refusal of other groups to convert. Positive values in the Indians' choice to convert to Methodism included the desire to possess material comforts such as houses, food, and clothing, and the chance to learn European skills such as reading and writing, farming and light industry.

These things must be seen against the background of environmental pressures; the encroachment of white settlers on Indian hunting grounds and the disappearance of game, debilitating drunkenness which left the Indians in debt to the traders and bereft of all their possessions, the high incidence of sickness and death resulting from contact with the white population and liquor. An important positive value was the emotional impact of the religion itself, at a time when many of the old practices and beliefs were dying out. In the Mississauga communities, the Indians did not have too much to lose from conversion. Even those who had a vested interest in the Ojibwa religion could maximize their benefits by becoming Methodist class leaders and local preachers, thereby retaining their positions of prestige, if not their prosperity. The chiefs of the small Mississauga groups had carried their Indians with them, or perhaps followed the consensus of opinion of the group; at any rate, there was not much risk involved to their positions in the decision to convert.

At Munceytown, on the other hand, where there were several chiefs, conversion was more of a gamble if the chief was not sure of his followers' support. In the western part of Ontario during the 1820's, the pressure on the land was not so great. The Indians still had some political and religious resources of their own. The same response to the missionaries was given in many places. Namely, that the Indians had a perfectly good religion of their own, and if God had wanted them to be Christian, he would have sent Jesus to them, but as it was, they did not need Jesus because they observed their religion faithfully. Traders also influenced the chiefs against accepting the missionaries, in order to maintain their liquor trade. The cost for these Indians of material comforts was too high at that time.

When Denke tried to convert the Ojibwa of the Lake St. Clair region in 1802, he got very little response, but then there was little incentive for the Indians, and there were few pressures on them. By the 1840's, the missionaries were beginning to have some value for these Indians.

The example of the benefits to be gained from conversion in such communities as the Credit and Grape Island was evident. Even before these
results were apparent, the Saugeen chief admitted that he was converting to Methodism because everyone else was; there was no profit for him
in being a hold-out and losing his share of the pie simply to retain his
independence.

Some of the chiefs wanted the benefits without the cost of commitment to Christianity, and requested education for their people without
conversion, but by the 1840's, pressure from the missionaries and the
government agents made it difficult for the chiefs to hold out against
Christianity. At Walpole Island, the chief finally invited the Church of
England to send a missionary. He realized, presumably, that it would be
more advantageous for him to be allied with a missionary of his selec-
tion or approval than to resist the advances of many groups without any
outside support. The Walpole Island chief entered into an alliance with
the Church of England missionary which yielded him and his people considerable benefits over the years. At St. Clair, where the chief had also
resisted conversion for many years, the chief's decision to ally with the
Methodists, which was probably based on similar reasoning and the fact
that many of his people were converting, was, however, an unfortunate
choice because it placed him in opposition to the agent who supported
the Church of England, and eventually lost him his job. By the 1840's,
as pressure from the Europeans surrounding the communities, and the
white people involved in the communities, grew stronger, the chiefs
really had very little choice but to accept missionaries. The chiefs tried
to make the best of the situation by selecting missionaries who could
support them. At Munceytown, for example, one group of Chippewas
joined with the Church of England, and the other Chippewa group with
the Methodists.

The only Indian groups to formally retain their own religion were
some of the Six Nations Indians, and some Oneida. The Oneida, who
followed the religion of Handsome Lake, were latecomers into Ontario,
and had an organized religious system. The Cayuga were the main group
to resist Christianity on the Grand River. The reason for this can only
be guessed at, not established. Geographically and structurally they
were separated from the other tribes. That is, they lived at the opposite
end of the river from the Mohawks, who had accepted Christianity first,
and they were in the opposite moiety to the Mohawks in the League
of the Iroquois, structurally most distant from the Mohawks. The

values of their religion were similar to those of Christianity in the emphasis on sobriety and morality, and they probably did not see the need to change their religion for their values to be acceptable to whites.

This approach to conversion as a social phenomenon might seem to ignore the role of the missionary as an agent of social change, and his influence on individuals. However, conversion of the individuals depends on the prospective convert's perceiving the personal benefits of conversion, as well as the benefits for the group. The missionaries, therefore, had to provide for the individual as much information as possible on the positive values of conversion, in order to achieve their goals. The successful innovator in religious matters would therefore need certain resources and attributes. There are certain obvious qualities he should have, such as an attractive personality, and an ability to speak the language or the willingness to learn. However many factors contributed to the success of the missionary: which missionary society he belonged to and the way it presented the message of Christianity, its relationship with the Government, and the success and personalities of his colleagues. It has been suggested that "the successful (i.e., acceptable) innovator is invariably some kind of hybrid, part inside, part outside the 'ordinary System' " (Wallman 1972). It is obvious that one of the most successful innovators in this area, whose work dominated the Methodist missions in the 1820's and 1830's, was a hybrid, both physically and socially. Peter Jones was half-Ojibwa, half-Welsh, he spoke Ojibwa and English, and he became an Indian chief and a missionary. His ability to be Indian with Indians and a missionary with missionaries, and perhaps more importantly, his ability to be a missionary with Indians and an Indian with missionaries, enabled him to accomplish very significant changes. Other missionaries who came closest to accomplishing the kinds of changes they were aiming for were the Moravian missionaries in the early days of the mission, and Andrew Jamieson on Walpole Island. These missionaries were not physical hybrids, but they performed many roles as missionaries, doctors, schoolteachers, farmers, politicians, etc. They learned the language and participated in community life with the Indians, being part of the community, but belonging also to the outside social system. The performance of a number of roles was an important factor in successful innovation, giving the missionary authority in many spheres of the social system. Successful performance of the "missionary role" did imply the performance of multiple roles, and of necessity, these included educational and economic roles as well as religious roles. It was not always necessary, however, for the missionary to play the roles himself if he was in charge of a team of people (schoolteachers, farmers, etc.) who were identified with the mission.

Many of the changes brought about by missionaries have been described, but it is very difficult to make a definitive assessment of the success of missionaries in Upper Canada, because their work was intertwined with that of the Government, and other agents of white society such as traders, and cannot be considered in isolation. This link with the Government, and the identification of the missionaries with the values of western society, has important implications and gives missionary roles an ambiguity, because government and missionary interests were not always identical. Government policies often militated against the success of missionary work. Although Sir John Colborne was inspired by the success of the Methodists to emulate their work, he was not backed up financially by his Government, and government intervention in communities that had been under Methodist control frequently caused conflict between missionary and government agent, and in consequence, the work suffered. The Government's subsequent policy to remove the Indians to Manitoulin Island, the refusal to give Indians any title to their lands, and in many cases, failure to inform the Indians about their rights, and exactly what security they could expect on their lands, failure to survey the land properly (Rice Lake) or according to agreement (Saugeen), kept the Indians in such a state of uncertainty that they did not improve their lands, and this impeded missionary work. In some cases improvements on the land made it more desirable for white people, and the Indians were more likely to lose it, or to be put under more pressure to move. Pressure to move was hard to resist, especially when the Indians were promised riches and luxury for the sale of their lands.

On the other hand, the identification of missionaries with the values of western society, and their roles as contact agents of that society, gave them interests similar to those of Government. Harold Cardinal writes that, "the church . . . worked hand in hand with existing government officials in plotting the life of the Indian . . . the government needed the church to control the Indians by persuading them to live peacefully on reservations. . . . " (1969:84—85). The evidence for Upper Canada does suggest that the missionaries made it easier for the Government to settle the Indians on reserves. They did collect the Ojibwa into communities and persuade them of the advantages of settled life, and the cultivation of the land, and the adoption of western religion, education, morality and life style. However, several of the Indian groups (Six Nations, Mohawks of the Bay of Quinte, Munsees, Moravians) already had a long-standing relationship with the British Government from whom they acquired land in the first place. It can be argued that the missionaries in Upper Canada did not destroy Indian culture, not because of any particular virtue possessed by these missionaries, but because much of Indian culture had already been destroyed, and what remained would not have been able to resist the general pressure from white settlement and society. A case can be made that missionaries helped the Indians to preserve the remnants of their culture. Without missionary intervention, the Indians might, according to Sir Francis Bond Head's prediction, have died out from disease, alcoholism, and accidents, poverty and malnutrition resulting from drunkenness, or from breeding with whites. There was quite extensive sexual activity between whites and Indians, but missionary morality did not accept extra-marital sexual relations, and this prevented much interbreeding.

In addition to this influence on the physical identity of the Indians, the missionaries also helped the Indians to reestablish their sociological identity. Missionaries collected or attracted the Indians in communities, and in several cases reserved land for the Indians, and the established communities that grew up under missionary care were better able to withstand the considerable pressure from Government to sell the land and move to Manitoulin Island in the late 1830's. The missionaries protected the Indians from the "bad" elements of the white population, and tried to overcome the dependency of the Indians on the Government.

The change from scattered hunting and gathering groups of people in the early days of the period, and the growth of rural, farming communities has been observed. Missionaries had a great impact on the Indians in the transitional phase they experienced from relative autonomy, to the loss of the land and dependence on the Government. Missionaries also had relative autonomy in this period, and could play more roles. The attempt to create "model" communities in the idealized image of the white man was successful for a brief period. Towards the middle of the nineteenth century, interest in the project seems to have waned as the work became more routine. As the government agents took over many of the roles previously played by missionaries, and as the Indians had been converted to Christianity in most communities, the need for many of the missionary roles gradually disappeared.

While this material and the analysis of it has been specific to Ontario over a certain period, similar conclusions might be drawn for other periods and in other contexts. It is interesting to note that in an analogous colonial situation, missionaries to the Khoi Khoin of South Africa played very similar roles, but as the sole contact agents during the nineteenth century did not compete with government agents for power and were able to promote more changes [this is discussed further in Graham (1968), and some comparative remarks can be found in Graham (1973)].

The influence of missionaries, or any change agent, varies. It can be positive or negative, advantageous or detrimental, depending on whose perspective is being considered, and on the situation itself. For example, some groups who refused to accept missionaries at one time, welcomed them as changes in the social and geographical environment altered their situation. Many variables operate in social change situations. There are the stated aims of particular groups and individuals, the characteristics of the innovator, the needs and perceptions of the people, and the social and geographical constraints of the environment. There is evidence of the effect of all these factors in the preceding account of missionaries as agents of change in Ontario from 1784 to 1867. The evidence is patchy due to the limitations of method and material discussed in the first chapter. It has been the objective of this book to demonstrate that processes of change have a logic of their own, that they are not the result of a straightforward amalgamation of two sets of values, nor can they be understood as a simple confrontation between missionaries and Indians.

APPENDIX I

Excerpt from *The Indian Chief* by Conrad Van Dusen (1867: 51-60) giving an account of the surrender of the Saugeen Peninsula.

LAND NOT ACCOUNTED FOR

PROMISES NOT FULFILLED – STRANGE PROCEEDINGS OF CAPTAIN ANDERSON – UNFAIR MEANS USED TO OBTAIN A SURRENDER OF LAND – TREATY SIGNED

The Indians in the Owen Sound country had previously surrendered to the Government a strip of land half a mile wide, extending from Owen Sound eighteen or twenty miles westward to the Saugeeng River, for which they got no returns. It was surveyed, and sold principally to land speculators, and of the sales of that land the Indians have got no account. But, notwithstanding the dissatisfaction they felt about this land surrender, still many of the most ignorant and indolent part of the tribe were elated with the prospects held out to them by the agents sent by the Indian Department, to negociate with them for the surrender of nearly the whole of their peninsula. They were told that from the sale of the land they would soon have a large income, that they would all be able to ride in carriages, roll in wealth, and fare sumptuously every day. Notwithstanding the previously broken promises and blasted hopes of former days, yet the credulous part of the tribe were elated with the prospect of being saved from penury; while others, remembering the past treatment, were sceptical about the future.

When proposals of this kind are made to the Indians, they generally pause to deliberate upon it; but no matter how much they hesitate at first, a little flattery, or coercion, will bring them into almost any favourite measure the Government may think fit to propose.

In August, 1854, Captain Anderson, Supt. Ind. Affrs., visited Owen Sound, and called a general council of the Indians, to obtain from them a surrender of their land. Many were unwilling to surrender any more, till the Department gave a satisfactory account of the sale of the land last ceded to them. Some remarked that they had surrendered one tract of land after another, that in some instances they had been paid only in promises, and that they remained as poor as ever.

After Captain Anderson had retired for a while from the council, in his absence the Indians concluded to make the desired surrender, but on certain conditions; and the council requested Chief Sawyer to state those conditions to Captain Anderson. So, when the captain came in the council to hear the result of their deliberations, the chief proceeded to state the conditions on which they had agreed to make the surrender; and then said, their other surrenders had been made in a loose way, and quite too indefinite; but these appeared to the captain quite too stringent and definite. Captain Anderson, in reply, expressed his disapprobation of the conditions; and said, "These conditions of surrender now proposed never originated in the brain of an Indian." Nevertheless the conditions were written down, and sent to the Department, by whom they were repudiated. Of course they were too definite to suit the Department.

I do not know whether Captain Anderson intended to hold Chief Sawyer alone responsible for the result of the deliberations of that council, or had some other object in view. He deviated from his usual course in such matters; for he requested Chief Sawyer to attach his name alone to the conditions proposed, which he did, and the document was sent by Captain Anderson to head quarters.

Chief Sawyer was willing to bear the responsibility, though this and other transactions of a similar character have, no doubt, caused the Indian Department to be strongly prejudiced against the chief. In Captain Anderson's letter to Mr. Oliphant, a few days after this council was held, he advises the Government to send on surveyors at once, and "assume a control over the reserve or peninsula." He states that "it may be argued, that the Indians have a deed or patent for this property; but even should such a deed in any way be valid, their guardians surely have authority over it," &c.

When he found that holding out promises to the Indians would not induce them to surrender their land, he advises the Government to coerce them, even if their deed of declaration is valid in law. What next?

When Mr. Oliphant, superintendent-general of Indians' affairs, came, two or three months after this, to treat with the Indians for the surrender of their peninsula, he passed by the band at Newash without even letting them know of his arrival, or the object of his visit, and proceeded about twenty miles to Saugeeng; and, as he states in his Report of the 3rd of November, 1854, addressed to Lord Elgin, and included in the copy of a dispatch from the Governor-General, the Earl of Elgin, to the Right Honourable Sir G. Grey, Bart., M.P., that "shortly after the chiefs of other bands arrived, and anxious not to allow them an opportunity of consulting even among themselves, or with Europeans, [he] called a general council at seven P.M., in the church at the Indian village, which was attended by the chiefs of the different bands and warriors of the Saugeeng Band." He also states that then he "opened the proceedings of the council." And as an inducement for the Indians to make the surrender, he adds, in the same Report, that he promised that the lands, when surveyed, should be sold by auction, that arrangements should be made, by which separate titles to farm lots should be granted by the Department to the Indians within their own reserves. He also, as a further inducement, promised that the chiefs should be "rewarded by his Excellency with medals." Perhaps Mr. Oliphant thought it was *fair* not to allow the Indians to have an opportunity to consult, even among themselves, in reference to the surrender of their lands. But the more intelligent part of them happened to think otherwise. And how Mr. Oliphant could suppose the council "was attended by the chiefs of the different bands," as he states in his Report, is another mystery; for there was not one chief from Colpoy's Bay that attended on that occasion, from first to last. And from Newash, they did not reach Saugeeng till the next day, after nearly all the arrangements had been completed. They arrived from Newash just in time to sign the treaty; and there is no doubt that many who did sign it would have done so, if it had been their death warrant. They knew nothing about the value of land, nor of the proper mode of transacting business. But they considered it unfair to hurry the business through, without even giving timely notice to the Indians at Newash and at Colpoy's Bay.

John Beaty was the only Indian from Colpoy's Bay, and only happened to be present; but he never was a chief, nor have we reason to suppose he ever will be, nor did he pretend to have any claim to the land or the annuities of that band. But when asked by Mr. Oliphant if he would represent the Colpoy's Bay Indians, he of course had no objections, and signed the treaty accordingly. This is the kind of legislation we often have in Indian affairs.

But if the Indians had been permitted to act upon the Resolution adopted by their General Council, October 30th, 1852, and allowed time to call together the chiefs and principal men from the three bands at Newash, Saugeeng, and Colpoy's Bay, in General Council; and then had Mr. Oliphant laid his business before them, they undoubtedly would have understood the matter much better, and arrangements would have been made much more intelligibly and satisfactorily. But this was not done. The deliberations were hurried through in a summary way. On the arrival of the Indians from Newash it was too late to propose any new arrangements; and two chiefs from the Newash Band could neither read nor write, and understood but few words in English. Under these circumstances, so far as Chief Sawyer was concerned, he made a virtue of necessity, and placed his name with the rest upon the document.

Mr. Oliphant having promised, as one condition of the surrender of their territory, as he states in his Report, that "arrangements should be made by which separate titles to farm lots should be granted by the Department to the Indians, within their own reserves;" they received this promise in good faith, and supposed each Indian in the tribe who had arrived at the age of twenty-one, would receive a deed for a farm lot, on which he could become an actual settler.

Chief Sawyer, as a member of the tribe, had no objections to surrender all the land unoccupied, which they did not require for farming purposes; for the benefit of the country he wished all the vacant land in the country occupied by white men or Indians. But while white men and black men, whether industrious or shiftless, whether frugal or prodigal, whether sober men or drunkards, could obtain deeds for land, the poor Indian has not been able to obtain a deed for one foot of his own land in Canada. It has been withheld from the red man, fearing he might be cheated out of it. How kind! We have all known black men, and white men too, cheated out of their farms, but not by Indians. Why not extend kindness also to them in the same way?

In closing the hurried business of their council for the surrender of their territory, the following document, having been prepared by Mr. Oliphant was presented, signed and sealed.

"SURRENDER OF THE SAUGEENG PENINSULA.

"We the chiefs, sachems, and principal men of the Indian tribes, resident at Saugeeng, Owen Sound, confiding in the wisdom and protecting care of our Great Mother across the big lake, and believing that our good father, his Excellency the Earl of Elgin and Kincardine, Governor General of Canada, is anxiously desirous to promote those interests which will most largely conduce to the welfare of his red children, have now being in full council assembled in presence of the superintendent-general of Indian affairs, and of the young men of both tribes agreed that it will be highly desirable for us to make a full surrender unto the crown of that peninsula known as the Saugeeng and Owen Sound Indian Reserve, subject to certain restrictions and reservations to be hereinafter let forth. We have therefore set our marks to this document, after having heard the same read to us, and do hereby surrender the whole of the above named tract of country bounded on the south by a straight line drawn from the Indian village of Saugeeng to the Indian village of Newash, in continuation of the northern limit of the narrow strip recently surrendered by us to the crown, and bounded on the north, east, and west by Georgian Bay and Lake Huron, the following reservations:—To wit.

"1st. For the benefit of the Saugeeng Indians we reserve all that block of land bounded on the west by a straight line running due north from the river Saugeeng at the spot where it is entered by a ravine immediately to the west of the village, and over which a bridge has recently been constructed. To the shore of Lake Huron, on the south by the aforesaid northern limit of the lately surrendered strip, on the east by a line drawn from a spot upon the coast at a distance of about nine miles and a half from the western boundary aforesaid, and running parallel thereto, until it touches the aforementioned northern limit of the recently surrendered strip. And we wish it to be clearly understood that we wish the peninsula at the mouth of the Saugeeng River to the west of the western boundary aforesaid to be laid out in town and park lots, and sold for our benefit without delay, and we also wish it to be understood that our surrender includes that parcel of land which is in continuation of the strip recently surrendered to the Saugeeng River. We do also reserve to ourselves that tract of land called Chiefs' Point, bounded on the east by a line drawn from a spot half a mile up the Sable River, and continued in a northerly direction to the bay, and upon all other sides by the lake.

"2nd. We reserve for the benefit of the Owen Sound Indians, all that tract bounded on the south by the northern limit of the continuation of the strip recently surrendered, on the northwest by a line drawn from the north-easterly angle of the aforesaid strip (as it was surrendered in 1851, in a north-easterly direction) on the south-east by the sound extending to the southern limit of the Changhnawaga settlement, on the north by a line two miles in length, and forming the said southern limit, and we also reserve to ourselves that tract of land called Cape Crocker, bounded on three sides by Georgian Bay, on the south-west side by a line drawn from the bottom of Noche-mowenaing Bay to the mouth of Sucker River, and we enclose in the aforesaid surrender, the parcel of land contained in the continuation to Owen Sound of the recently surrendered strip aforesaid.

"3rd. We do reserve for the benefit of the Colpoy's Bay Indians, in the presence of John Beattie, who represents the tribe at this council, a block of land containing 6,000 acres, and including their village, and bounded on the north by Colpoy's Bay.

"All which reserves we hereby retain to ourselves and our children in perpetuity; and it is agreed that the interest of the principal sum arising out of the sale of our lands, be regularly paid to them so long as there are Indians left to represent our tribe, without diminution, at half-yearly periods.

"And we hereby request the sanction of our great father the Governor General to this surrender, which we consider highly conducive to our general interest.

"Done in council at Saugeeng this thirteenth day of October, 1854. It is understood that no islands are included in this surrender.

(Signed and sealed,)

"JOHN (symbol) KADNHGEKWUN (seal)
ALEXANDER (symbol) MADWAYOSH "
JOHN (symbol) MONEDROWAR "
JOHN (symbol) THOMAS WAHBADICK "
PETER (symbol) JONES "
DAVID SAWYER "
JOHN H. BEATTIE "
THOMAS (symbol) PAHAHMORH ".
JOHN (symbol) MADWASHERMINT "
JOHN (symbol) JOHNSTON "
JOHN AUNJEGAHBOWH "
JAMES NEWASH "
THOMAS (symbol) WAHBADICK "
CHARLES KEISICK "

(Signed,) "L. OLIPHANT,
Superintendent-General Indian Affairs,
PETER JACOBS,
Missionary, witness.
(Signed) JAS. ROSS, M.P.P.,
C. RANKIN, P.L.S.,
A. McNABB,
Crown Land Agent."

APPENDIX II

Descriptions of Ojibwa Religion

George Copway

However absurd may have been our notions of the multiplied deities of the earth, yet, as a general thing, the Ojibways, as well as many others, believed that there was but one Great Spirit, who made the world; they gave him the name of good or benevolent; *kesha* is benevolent, *monedoo* is spirit; Ke-sha-mon-e-doo. They supposed he lived in the heavens; but the most of the time he was in the *sun.* They said it was from him they received all that was good through life, and that he seldom needs the offering of his red children, for he was seldom angry.

They also said he could hear all his children, and see them. He was the author of all things that they saw, and made the other spirits that were acknowledge by the Ojibways. It was said that these other spirits took special care of the various departments of nature. The god of the *hunter* was one who presided over the animals; the god of *war* was one who controlled the destinies of men; the god of *medicine* was one who presided over the herbs of the earth. The fishes had their god, and there was another over the moon and stars!

"Millions of spiritual creatures walk the earth
Unseen, both when we sleep and when we wake."

There was one unappeasable spirit, called the Bad Spirit, Mah-je-mah-ne-doo. He, it was thought, lived under the earth; and to him was attributed all that was not good, bad luck, sickness, even death. To him they offered sacrifices more than to any other spirit, of things most dear to them. There were three things that were generally offered to the Bad Spirit, viz., a dog, whiskey, and tobacco, — fit offerings, with the exception of the poor dog. The poor dog was painted red on its paws, with a large stone and five plugs of tobacco tied about its neck; it was then sunk in the water; while the beating of the drum took place upon the shore, and words were chanted to the Bad Spirit.

The whiskey was thus offered to the Bad Spirit: — When the Indians were seated around the wigwam, or on the grass, and the person who dealt out the whiskey had given all the Indians a dram, then the devil was to have his share; it was poured on the ground, and if it went down quickly, it was thought he accepted the offering.

Fire-water was sometimes poured out near the head of the graves of the deceased, that their spirits might drink with their former friends. I have often seen them sit around the grave, and, as they drank, make mention of the name of their dead, and pour some whiskey on the ground.

Our religion consisted in observing certain ceremonies every spring. Most of the Ojibways around us used to come and worship the Great Spirit with us at Rice Lake. At this festival a great many of the youth were initiated into the medical mysteries of the nation. We were taught the virtues of herbs, and the various kinds of minerals used in our medicine. I will here describe the Me-tae-we-gah-mig, or Grand Medicine Lodge. It was a wigwam 150 feet long and 15 feet wide. The clan of medicine men and women alone were allowed to be inside, at each sitting, with their medicine badge, on each side of the wigwam. Then there were four old men who took the lead in singing, and beating the drum, as they stood near the centre. Before them were a company who were to take degrees. There were four grades in the institution. A medicine man is the most important personage in the worship of the Indians. He is the high priest of the ceremony, and keeps all the records of traditions and emblems. He is also the keeper of the great bag which is full of herbs, which is opened only when lectures are given for to illustrate them.

He is supposed to possess a great power over man and beast, and, therefore, to court his favour was an object worthy the consideration of young men.

After the singing commenced, the whole company arose and danced, as they moved from one end of the wigwam to the other. As they go round, one-half of them cast their heads down upon their bosoms, as if affected by the medicine, which was kept in small skins, and which they pretended to thrust at each other: this was done to deceive the ignorant. These forms were continued several days. The party to be made medicine men and women looked on in the meantime, to see what they would have to do themselves. Then they are taken to another place with our medicine men, and are taught the science of medicine. After receiving instructions, another day was allotted to give them instruction on morality. They were advised on various subjects. All were to keep silence, and endeavour to retain what they were taught. I will here give some of the sayings of our medicine men: —

"If you are a good hunter, warrior, and a medicine man, when you die you will have no difficulty in getting to the far west in the spirit land."

"Listen to the words of your parents, never be impatient, then the Great Spirit will give you a long life."

"Never pass by any indigent person without giving him something to eat. Owh wah-yah-bak-mek ke-gah-shah-w a-ne-mig — the Spirit that sees you will bless you."

"If you see an orphan in want, help him; for you will be rewarded by his friends here, or thanked by his parents in the land of spirits."

"If you own a good hunting dog, give it to the first poor man who really needs it."

"When you kill a deer, or bear, never appropriate it to yourself alone, if others are in want; never withhold from them what the Great Spirit has blessed you with."

"When you eat, share with the poor children who are near you, for when you are old they will administer to your wants."

"Never use improper medicine to the injury of another, lest you yourself receive the same treatment."

"When an opportunity offers, call the aged together, and provide for them venison properly cooked, and give them a hearty welcome; then the gods that have favoured them will be your friends." (Copway 1851: 27–31)

Peter Jones

The various tribes of the Ojebway nation scattered along the shores of the great lakes universally believe in the existence of one Supreme Being; whom they call *Kechemunedoo,* which literally signifies *the Great Spirit,* or Kezha-munedoo, the Benevolent or Merciful Spirit. Believing Him to abound in love and mercy towards his creatures, they suppose him too exalted to concern Himself with the follies of poor earthly beings, whose existence lasts only as it were for a day, his chief care being that of supplying their daily wants. *Munedoo* means a spirit, either good or bad. In order to designate the character or nature of the spirit, they use the prefixes, as in the words above-mentioned.

They also believe in the existence of an evil spirit, whom they call *Mahje-munedoo.* This spirit, they imagine, possesses power to injure any who dare to offend him; and, in order to retain his friendship and appease his anger, some have been known to offer sacrifice to him, so that he might not bring upon them death, illness, or bad luck in hunting.

They, moreover, believe that there are innumerable subordinate deities, or spirits, who have particular control over the affairs of this world. For instance, they believe that there is one god who has the charge of *game,* another who presides over the *fish* and the water, another who controls the winds and the storms, and another who watches over the vegetable world.

These imaginary deities become the objects of their invocations when they are so circumstanced as to require their blessing. For instance, if an Indian wishes for success on a hunting excursion, he will direct his offering and prayer to the god who presides over the deer, the bear, or the beaver, (a wonderful gamekeeper he must be,) that success may attend him; or, if he desires to catch many fish, or have a prosperous voyage, he will sacrifice to the god of the waters. I have known an Indian kill a black dog and throw it into the lake, that he might meet with no disaster whilst on his voyage. In this way the poor dark-minded Indian ignorantly worships the creatures of his own imagination.

The sun, moon, and stars are also adored as gods. At the rising of the sun the old chiefs and warriors chant their hymns of praise to welcome his return; and, at his going down they thank him for the blessing of light and heat during the day. When a visible eclipse of the sun takes place, the poor Indians are thrown into the greatest alarm. They call it the sun's dying, and suppose that he actually dies. In order to assist in bringing him to life again, they stick coals of fire upon the points of their arrows, and shoot them upwards into the air, that by these means the expiring sun may be reanimated and rekindled. The moon and stars are reverenced for the light they give by night, enabling the lonely wanderer to travel in the absence of the sun. . . .

In addition to their belief in the existence of these general gods, each *pow-wow conjuror* and *medicine man* has his personal or familiar gods, which are of his own imagining. The method they take to obtain the favour of these is by fasting and watching. The Indian youth from the age of ten to manhood are encouraged by their parents and the old people to fast, with the promise that if they do they will entertain them in the evening by the relation of one of their traditions or tales. Inspired with the hope of gaining favour with some god, and looking forward to the promised reward at the end of the day, they rise before the sun, take a piece of charcoal, which they pound to powder, and with it blacken their faces, the girls only blackening the upper part. During their fast they abstain from all food and drinks; towards sunset they wash their faces and then eat a little broth or soup which has been prepared for them; in this way they go on for several successive days.

(Jones 1859:83–87)

An Indian Feast

Having been informed that the Indians were about to attend a Medai Kechewegoondewin, or Conjurers great feast, I determined if practicable, to witness the ceremony: first, for my own satisfaction; and secondly, with the view of furnishing the readers of the Guardian with the particulars.

This feast was given, and the ceremony attended to, in order to initiate two Indian children into the order of Medai or Conjurors, or as some writers on Indian customs have been pleased to designate this class of men, the "priesthood". The ground selected for this occasion, was a sandy spot on the bank of the St. Clair River, about half a mile distant from the Mission house, close by the graves of the sleeping fathers of this once numerous tribe; a spot for which the Indians generally have a great veneration.

Early in the morning of the day appointed, the women assembled, with implements suitable for their labour, and levelled the ground, carefully removing all the small stumps and roots, and making the same perfectly smooth. Small stakes, at regular distances, were driven into the ground, enclosing a plot of about fifty feet in length and 25 in breadth, to these at the height of about 5 feet were tied with bark, long poles, to which were hung canoe-sails, tent cloths, blankets, etc.; thus enclosing the whole, and excluding observations and entrance, except at each end where an opening of about 6 feet was left. In the centre were driven two strong stakes about two feet apart, to each of which was tied a wooden image resembling the human figure, the head being loose in order to admit the body which was below, to be filled, as it was on this occasion, with kahshkekeh or medicine prepared from roots, barks, leaves, etc.

About noon, nine kettles, holding from two to four pails full, were placed before the company; some few were served from the same in tin pans but the greater part, unceremoniously, and in no small quantities, helped themselves, and the pork, hams, venison, ducks, squirrels, raccoons, bears meat and other game being boiled to shreds they found no difficulty in dispensing with forks, and in many cases with knives also, pulling the food to pieces, and appearing to comprehend the old proverb, "fingers were made before forks:" nor were they less forgetful of the Indian maxim "eat all that is set before you:" for it can scarcely be said the kettles were successively emptied, — but rather simultaneously; the company amounted to between one hundred and fifty and two hundred. This evidently gratifying part of the ceremony being ended, a select party consisting of the Medai or Conjurors, retired to the woods and spent nearly an hour in singing to the spirits; while the women fetched some straw and spread it around the enclosure, and made some other necessary arrangements. As the evening shadows closed in, the fires were lighted, one at each entrance, and the company began to take their seats. After some time, for Indian movements are generally very deliberately performed, all were seated, and one of the Medai took the Tatewaegun or drum and commenced slowly beating it at intervals of nearly a second, as a signal that all was now in readiness; upon which the men, women and children arose, and took their places in rows or rank within the enclosure; this done, the Medai began to beat more lively, two women accompanying the sound of the drum with the sheshegwun or rattle, while they struck a song and all began to dance; this consisted in a gentle and not ungraceful movement of the body, and occasionally a step or two with the feet. So regular and uniform is the movement and so grotesque the appearance, each being wrapped in a new white blanket, on which being a beautiful clear night, the moon, which was full, cast her silver light and gave a striking effect to the scene, that an observer can scarcely believe but that the ground on which he stands is in motion, and almost imagine himself to be moving in unison with the company. There were present nine male and two female Medin, the drum was alternately beat and the singing led by each about half an hour, while all joined in the chorus; the men occasionally singing softly, unaccompanied by the females, and at other times having pleasant voices, they produce, unassociated with the recollection of paganism, not unpleasing music. This was the introduction to the ceremony of initiation. A little boy about six and a little girl about seven years of age were the subjects; these, who had accompanied the Medai to the words, now joined in the singing, and took a prominent place in the dance. After this dance, the drum having been beat by each Medai, all took their seats, and each took a dram of whiskey: but two however showed signs of intoxication, and these never attempted to join in the exercises; assigning to me on enquiry, as a reason why they did not, "we are too drunk".

A blanket was now spread in the centre, and the two children were seated thereon, with their faces towards the images before mentioned; and pieces of blue and red cloth, containing about a quarter of a yard each were spread at their feet. Two women took their places behind them, in the parts they would be required to act in the ceremony. The oldest man in the tribe arose and spoke about fifteen minutes, addressing himself first to the men, then to the women, and lastly to the children. Exhorting them to hold fast on the religion of their fathers; to be patient in enduring hardships; and urging on the children to observe mahgahtawin or blacking and fasting: (a religious ceremony) and closed by promising them, should they observe what he said, beards as white as his, which was silvered over with age and limbs as strong therewith: he then began a song in praise of the children seated in the centre, the chorus, in which all joined being: "Oh, Oh nejahnesun. ne nejahnesun" which ended all at once arose, crying "Wah wah wah" and commenced dancing and moving around the enclosure in file, keeping in their movements the most regular order, and timing their steps to the drums, rattles and vocal sounds. This exercise, which appeared to be a compliment to the children, all the song being in their praise, continued about fifteen or twenty minutes, and again all resumed their seats.

The Medai now arose, all the rest remaining seated in silence, and each took his or her kahshkekeh mahahkemoot, or medicine pouch, being an otter skin, containing from fifty to a hundred very small parcels of mahshkekeh, or medicine used in conjuring, consisting of roots, leaves, bark, cinnamon cloves, tobacco, a small wooden box, some mekis, or sea shells, a wooden snake, some porcupine quills, a mink or squirrel skin, also full of medicine, atahpejegun, or cord to tie prisoners in war, a sheshegwun, or rattle used in curing the sick; and a variety of other small articles — and hung it in the belt around the waist. The chief Medai taking the lead, the others following, walked slowly and majestically around the enclosure several times, the chief Medai pressing on them to attend to their duty on this occasion; after which each took his pouch from the belt in which it hung, and, singing, kept the head of the skin moving up and down, thus beating time to their song. In a few minutes, continuing singing, they moved in file dancing towards the two children, carrying their skins in both hands, and giving them a gently undulating movement, similar to that of a snake in motion: each as he arrived presented the head of the skin to one and then to the other of the children's breasts, crying, "Hahwah yahwah." and at each presentation the women threw the children on their faces, raising them again for the next until the last, when the children were both left on their faces as if dead. All now uttered as loudly as possible, "Wah wah wah" and quickly retreated in haste, as if afraid, to the end of the enclosure; the women, at the same time stooping down and applying their mouths to the ears of the children, called aloud, "Ahwah ahwah ahwah" repeating these sounds five times; and pointing north, east, south and west, and lastly into the ground, again cried, "Wah wah wah" and raised the children to a sitting posture. The Medai during this time continued singing and walking slowly around the enclosure until they arrived again opposite the children, where they all stood still with their mouths open, and the chief Medai took from his pouch a root, and breaking it into small pieces put into each Medai's mouth a piece, which was chewed as they danced around. On arriving at the children they successively spat a little of the juice on the breast, on each side the neck, and on the back of each of the children; walking around once more, they each took up the pieces of cloth which laid by the children, and muttered some words too low to be distinguished, and retired to the end of the ground. Here they commenced singing and taking their skins, gave them the undulating motion before mentioned; then they proceeded to the children from whom they retreated in haste, and fell one over the other at the entrance of the enclosure. In a little time they arose, placed themselves in a row, and looking directly upwards, their heads being thrown back as far as possible, each holding in his finger and thumb a small piece of mahshkekeh, he put it five times into his own mouth, at each time crying "Yahahwah, Yahahwah, Yahahwah" and pointing to the four points and into the ground as before mentioned, they ran and fell at the other end of the encampment.

Each Medai now arose and made a speech, declaring the children to be regularly received into their community and to be constituted Medai, and that they should in future have the privilege of joining in every Medaiwegoontewin, and enjoining on each other to embrace every opportunity of instructing them in the wisdom of the Medai and promising them if these children endeavour to become wise, and attend to mahkahtiwin, (blacking or fasting) they would always own them as brethren among the Medai. The children were now led around the ground by their attendant women, and their right hands presented to every one present, the women shewing to every one a small sea shell; after which all joined in singing and dancing. The night was spent in drinking whiskey, and the morning found them as drunk as the accursed fire water could make them.

J. EVANS, St. Clair Rapids 18th Dec. 1834

(CG, January 28, 1835:45)

APPENDIX III

Community Rules: Moraviantown, Munceytown, Grape Island, the Credit.

Moraviantown

We whose names are hereunto subscribed do solemnly and sincerely agree among ourselves on the following rules and regulations, viz:

1. Everyone who wants to live with us must adore and worship God alone.
2. None shall live with us who will go to other places to feasts and dances.
3. None who will bring rum or whiskey into our town to get drunk, or to make others drunk, or who will go to other places to get drunk.
4. None who keeps a whore, or seduces another man's wife.
5. No man who forsakes his wife, saving for cause of fornication, nor woman who leaves her husband (can abide among us).
6. No son or daughter who abuses their parents (likewise none who abuse and attack his teachers to revenge his bad heart on them).
7. None that steals.
8. None that has poison or knows of it, none that uses beson witchcraft, or such like things.
9. None that will doctor or be doctored after the wild Indian manner.
10. None that paint, shave, shear or dress themselves as the heathen do, wearing plumes or feathers, hanging wampum and silver truck about them, nor play moccasin, cards and the like.
11. None that has a Chief's or Captain's medal or silver.
12. None that tell stories of another, of poison, night-walking and the like, and cannot prove it (the accused shall not live among us. But if he is found a liar, we will consider him as a tool of the devil who wants to hinder our love, and put him away from us).
13. We will all keep the Lord's day, and not work or go a hunting on such days, works of charity and necessity excepted. And we do further covenant, promise and agree, that if we (ourselves) or any of (among) us shall transgress and willfully and knowingly transgress the above rules, and after having been repeatedly admonished, shall continue to act contrary thereto, we will peaceably and quietly leave the place. In witness whereof we have hereunto set our hands.

(Gray 1956:110 from document in M.A.)

Muncey

1. Spirituous liquors are strictly prohibited.
2. The Indians are to be called together early in the morning:
    viz.   In summer at 4 O'Clock
           In winter at 6 O'Clock
    And after time given for dressing, they will meet and talk over their working arrangements, then proceed to prayers, take breakfast and commence their work under the direction of the farmer, aided by faithful Indians to direct the operations incident to any work of a *general* nature.
3. Two days in the week is allotted for hunting parties. But the men are not to be accompanied by their wives or children.
    The party going out on a *Monday* shall return on *Wednesday* evening,
    And the party going out on *Thursday* morning shall return on *Saturday* evening.
4. As the Indian families are encumbered with many *Dogs* that do no good; but destroy provisions useful to the owners. It is therefore considered, that one *Dog* for each family would answer every good purpose.

Done at the village of Colborne this 1st day of January, 1831.
    J.B. Clench
For the guidance of all concerned.
    That part of the preceding Regulation which directs going to prayers, applies only to those who have embraced the Christian Religion.
                                                                (RG10, vol. 47)

Grape Island

1. At the sound of the horn, in the morning at 5 o'clock in winter and 4 o'clock in summer, all to arise.
2. At half past 7 o'clock in winter, and half past 6 o'clock in summer, to breakfast. Dinner at half past 12 o'clock, and supper at 5 o'clock. The bell to be rung an hour before, and at the time of sitting down at table.
3. 9 o'clock P.M. Horn to sound for being at home to prepare for rest.

                              J.B. BENHAM (Jan. 22nd. 1830)

                              (CG, Feb. 13, 1830:99)

Credit

GOVERNMENT

1st. According to our ancient customs, the Indians of this village, shall be governed by Chiefs, at present three, one of whom shall be called the Head Chief or Keche-Ookemah, who shall have the supreme authority. It shall be his duty to preside in Councils — to see that the Laws are duly executed and observed — and to call councils when he deems it necessary, or when he is requested to do so by three or more resident householders. He is in all cases to govern according to law, and in no case to enforce any Regulation till it regularly becomes a law by receiving the sanction of the Council.

2nd. In case of the sickness, absence, or death of the Head Chief till a successor be elected, the second or war chief shall act in his place, and shall have full authority and act as head chief for the time being.

3rd. According to the old customs of our nation the Chiefs shall be chosen by a majority of our people, and shall retain their office during life; except in cases hereafter provided for.

4th. When a chief is to be chosen, publick notice must be given at least one month before the council meets for that purpose.

5th. The chiefs shall appoint a Mezhenahway or secretary, who shall keep the publick accounts, transcribe and keep the laws and regulations made by the councils and other publick documents, and perform all the duties of a private secretary.

6th. The Chiefs shall act as judges in all trials for debt, theft, drunkenness etc. or other offences against the laws and customs of our nation.'

7th. All writs, executions etc., shall be in the name of the Head Chief for the time being. When the chiefs act in a judicial capacity the head chief shall preside, but the sentence shall be a majority of voices. In trials when one or both of the parties request it, the chiefs shall cause a jury of six men to be called; but when the parties do not demand a jury, the chiefs may decide the cause alone.

8th. There shall be one Keche tah koonewa weneneh, and one tahkoonewaweneneence, whose duty it shall be to keep the peace, and to execute the writs, executions and summonses issued by the chief. These shall be chosen annually. But in case of neglect of duty or other misconduct, the chiefs shall have authority to dismiss either or both of them and order a new appointment to be made.

9th. The chiefs shall hold a council or court, four times in the year, viz:— 1st Wednesday in March, June, September and December, for the trial of offences committed against the laws and regulations of this village.

LAWS RELATING TO VARIOUS OFFENCES

1st. Any Indian inhabitant convicted of stealing shall restore fourfold, or at the discretion of the chiefs, if they think a less amount sufficient according to the circumstances of the case. For a repetition of the crime the offender shall be punished at the discretion of the Chiefs and Council.

2nd. Any one assaulting or beating another shall be fined at the discretion of the chiefs.

3rd. For slander the offender shall make such amends to the injured person as the chiefs shall direct.

4th. For bearing false witness, injuring a neighbour's property by fire, by throwing down his fences, killing or wounding his cattle or offences of the like kind, the offender shall be punished by fine or by banishment as the chiefs and council shall determine.

5th. Young persons who are disobedient to their parents, disorderly in their conduct, or otherwise misbehave to the injury of the publick shall be corrected at the discretion of the chiefs, either by their parents, or by the officers of justice.

GENERAL COUNCILS

A General Council of the whole nation in the village (two-thirds at least of resident householders shall be present) shall be held on the first day of January in every year, except when that falls on the Sabbath, then the day preceding the first of January; for the purpose of regulating the affairs of the nation, and choosing publick officers for the ensuing year. These councils shall be conducted according to our old customs, the chief presiding.

At these general councils any new law or regulation may be made by a vote of the majority; and any old law repealed by a vote of two-thirds.

To this Council the chiefs themselves shall be amenable, and for great offences, gross immorality, or notorious incapacity, may by a vote of two-thirds, be deposed, and a new chief or chiefs chosen.

OCCASIONAL COUNCILS

The occasional councils shall have no power to make or repeal laws. They may regulate all such things relating to the general improvement and welfare, as are not otherwise expressly provided for by law, and in certain cases in conjunction with the chiefs fix the degree of punishment to be inflicted on offenders. The occasional councils shall compose at least one chief and ten or more house holders.

The following Regulations shall be subject to the control of the occasional councils:

1st. All our lands, timber, and fishery shall be held as publick property, and no person shall be allowed to sell, lease or give any part of the lands, timber or fishery, unless granted by the council for the general benefit of our people.

2nd. All our people shall have full liberty to cut timber for their own use upon any part of the Reserve; and also to fish on the same.

3rd. No person among us shall have liberty to take up land or town lots without permission from the chiefs.

4th. The lands which have been allotted to families, shall be possessed by them and their descendents forever. But in case of neglecting to make improvements on them, in three years from the time such allotments were made, shall forfeit their right and claims on such lands, and be subject to the control of the councils.

5th. Our people shall have the liberty with the advice of the chiefs, to exchange their lots and to sell their improvements to one another.

6th. No dwelling house shall be built in the village less than 18 by 24 feet of hewed logs, which shall be erected under the control of the councils and a certain sum appropriated for that purpose of the publick funds.

7th. No stranger shall become resident in the village without the permission of the chiefs in council.

8th. No person among us shall be allowed to harbour or receive as residents into their houses, any disorderly person or persons except in cases of distress.

9th. No one shall be allowed to leave wood or timber in the streets of the village; nor to suffer any filth or dead carcasses to remain within the bounds of the village. But it shall be the duty of all householders to see that the village is perfectly free from all filth and dirt, which is necessary in order to preserve health in the place.

REGULATIONS CONCERNING THE FISHERY

1st. No person belonging to the village shall fish in the River Credit, on Saturday and Sunday nights, during the fall run of salmon.

2nd. No person shall give permission to any unauthorized person to fish or to take such to fish with him; unless it be thought expedient at a future council.

CONCERNING LABOR ON ROADS

1st. Each man belonging to the village or residing within the limits of the Reserve shall work six days in each and every year on the publick roads, or shall be subject to pay the sum of two shillings and sixpence currency per each day. Eight hours shall be allowed for a day's work.

2nd. Every yoke of oxen and every span of horses in the village shall work two days in each year, and every single horse one day in a year; or pay the above sum.

THE DUTY OF OVERSEERS OF ROADS, ETC.

1st. It shall be the duty of overseers of publick roads after receiving an order from the occasional councils, to warn the men to work on such parts of the publick roads as shall be directed by the council, and to keep an account of the number of days and hours that each man works.

2nd. It shall also be the duty of road masters to see that no obstructions are put in the streets of the village or in any of the publick roads; and to see that no filth, as the offalls of fish, and dead carcasses, etc., are allowed to remain in the village.   (RG10, vol. 46)

KEY TO NAMES

Aisance, John	Chief, Coldwater 1820s, Beausoleil Island; d.1847.
Anderson, T.G.	Superintendent, Coldwater, 1829-1837; Indian Superintendent (northern), 1837-1845; Chief Superintendent (Toronto), 1845-1858.
Brant, John	Indian Superintendent, Six Nations, 1828-1832.
Brant, Joseph	War Chief, Six Nations, 1783-1807.
Carey, John	Schoolteacher, Muncey, 1825-1828; Church of England missionary, Walpole Island, 1843-1844.
Case, William	General Superintendent Methodist Indian missions, 1826-1833; Methodist missionary, Alnwick; d.1856.
Claus, Powles	Chief, Tyendinaga, 1850s.
Claus, Col. William	Deputy Superintendent General Indian Affairs, 1799-1826.
Clench, J.B.	Indian Superintendent, Caradoc and Moravians, 1830-1854.
Colborne, Sir. John	Lieutenant-Governor Upper Canada, 1828-1836.
Coleman, James	Church of England missionary, Walpole Island, 1841-1843.
Copway, George	Rice Lake chief, Methodist missionary.
Darling, Maj.-Gen. H.C.	Deputy Superintendent General Indian Affairs, 1826-1828; Superintendent General Indian Affairs, 1828-1831.
Davis, Thomas	Mohawk chief, Six Nations, c.1822.
Denke, Christian	Moravian missionary, 1801-1818.
Douse, John	Methodist missionary, Grand River, c.1834.
Du Ranquet, Fr.	Roman Catholic missionary, Walpole Island, 1844-1849.
Elliot, Adam	Church of England missionary, Coldwater, 1833-1835; New England Company missionary, Grand River, 1840; d.1878.

Evans, James	Methodist missionary, St. Clair, 1834- ?
Flood, Richard	Church of England missionary, Muncey, 1835-1838; Oneida, 1846- ?
Gilmour, John	New England Company missionary, Chemong, 1837-1868.
Givins, James	Indian Agent, York, 1797; Superintendent, York, 1816-1830; Chief Superintendent, Toronto, 1830-1837.
Givins, Saltern	Church of England missionary, Tyendinaga, 1831-1851.
Glenelg, Lord	Secretary of State for Colonial Department, 1835-1839.
Head, Sir Francis Bond	Lieutenant Governor Upper Canada, 1836-1838.
Henry, George	Interpreter at St. Clair, ? - 1840.
Herkimer, William	Methodist missionary, Newash 1844; Beausoleil Island c.1847; Rice Lake 1855.
Heyland, Mr.	Methodist missionary, Six Nations, c.1847.
Hill, Abraham	Methodist chief, Bay of Quinte Mohawks, c.1834.
Hill, John	Mohawk chief, Bay of Quinte, 1850s.
Hough, William	New England Company missionary, Six Nations, 1844-1847.
Ironside, George	Indian Superintendent, Amherstburg 1830-1845; Indian Superintendent, northern Superintendency, 1845-1863.
Jacobs, Philip and Christian	Chiefs at New Fairfield, c.1840s & 1860s.
Jamieson, Andrew	Church of England missionary, Walpole Island, 1845-1885.
Jarvis, Col. William P.	Chief Superintendent, Toronto, 1837-1845.
Jennesseaux, Br.	Roman Catholic missionary, Walpole Island, 1844-1849.
Johnson, Sir John	Superintendent General, 1782-1828.
Jones, Peter	Methodist missionary and Credit chief; d.1856.

Jones, Polly	Peter's sister.
Jones, John	Schoolteacher, Credit, 1830s, Peter's brother.
Jones, William	Agent, Stony Point, 1831-1843.
Keating, J.W.	Assistant Superintendent, Walpole Island and St. Clair, 1839-1844.
Kegedonce	Chief, Saugeen c.1820s, Newash 1840s.
Kempt, Sir James	Commander of the Forces, Governor, 1828-1830.
Kezicks, Charles	Interpreter, Newash, c.1851.
Lugger, Robert	New England Company missionary, Grand River, 1827-1837.
Martin, Squire	Chief, Mud Lake, ? - 1842.
McKay, William	Resident Superintendent, Montreal, 1830-1832.
McKee, Col. Alexander	Deputy Superintendent General, Indian Affairs, 1794-1799.
Mishebishee, James	Chief, St. Clair, ? - 1848.
Morley, Rev.	New England Company missionary, Grand River, 1823-1824.
Nangi	Chief, St. Clair region, c.1800.
Nelles, Abraham	New England Company missionary, Grand River, 1831 - ?
Nogee, Peter	Chief, Mud Lake, 1842-1858.
Obadiah, John	Church of England catechist, Grand River, c.1842; d.1872.
Onim	Medicine man, Muncey, c.1816.
Otemekoo	Chippewa chief, Muncey, 1820s.
Paudash, George	Chief, Rice Lake, 1820s; d.1870.
Pazhekeshikquashkum	Chief, Walpole Island, c.1829.
Richardson, James	Methodist missionary, Credit, 1827.
Ryerson, E.	Methodist missionary, Credit, 1826.
Saco, Peter	Chief, Colpoy's Bay, 1840s.
Sawyer, David	Interpreter, chief, Methodist missionary, Saugeen and Newash, c.1846, son of Joseph.

Sawyer, Joseph	Chief, Credit 1830s; d.1864.
Schuyler, Moses	Chief, Oneida, c.1846.
Scott, Jonathan	Methodist missionary, St. Clair, 1840s.
Scott, Richard	New England Company missionary, Mud Lake, 1828-1837.
Sensemann, Gottlob	Moravian missionary, 1792-1800.
Simpson, John	Chief, Grape Island, 1820s; Alnwick, 1850s.
Slight, Benjamin	Methodist missionary, Credit, 1836.
Snake, Capt.	Munsee chief, Muncey, c. 1835.
Snake, William	Chief, Snake Island, Lake Simcoe, 1820s - ?
Stinson, Joseph	General Superintendent of Methodist Missions, 1833-1840.
Strachan, John	Archdeacon of York 1827; Bishop at Toronto 1839.
Stuart, George Okill	Church of England missionary to Mohawks, 1813 - ?
Stuart, John	Church of England missionary to Mohawks, 1784-1812.
Sunday, John	Chief, Methodist missionary, Alnwick, 1820s; d.187
Torry, Alvin	Methodist missionary, Grand River, 1822-1827.
Turkey, George	Munsee chief, Muncey, 1820s.
Turner, Thomas	Methodist missionary, St. Clair, 1832-1834.
Van Dusen, Conrad	Methodist missionary, Saugeen.
Vogler, Jesse	Moravian missionary, 1835-1865.
Wabadick, John T.	Chief, Newash, 1840s.
Wawanosh, David	Schoolteacher and chief, St. Clair, son of Joshua.
Wawanosh, Joshua	Chief, St. Clair, 1830s; d. 1871.
Westbrook	Munsee Chief, Muncey, 1820s.
Wilson, Edmund	Church of England missionary (C.M.S.), St. Clair, 1868-1870.
Yellowhead	Chief, Narrows, 1820s; Lake Simcoe, 1830s; Rama, 1840s.
Zeisberger, David	Moravian missionary, 1792-1798.

KEY TO ABBREVIATIONS

Journals

CA & J   Christian Advocate and Journal.

CEG   Canadian Ecclesiastical Gazette.

CG   Christian Guardian.

MI   Missionary Intelligencer and Religious Miscellany. United Brethren.

MM   Methodist Magazine (New York).

NEC   Reports, etc. Corporation for the Promoting and Propagating of the Gospel of Jesus Christ in New England.

PA   Periodical Accounts. United Brethren.

SPG   Reports. Society for the Propagation of the Gospel in Foreign Parts.

UBSPG   Proceedings of the Society for the Propagation of the Gospel among the Heathen. United Brethren.

WAR   Annual Reports. Methodist Episcopal Church Missionary Society in Canada.

WMN   Wesleyan Missionary Notices.

Manuscript Collections

CMS   Wilson Letters. Church Missionary Society.

MMN   Methodist Missionary Notices.

RG10   Record Group 10, Indian Affairs Papers.

SJ   Jennesseaux and Du Ranquet Letters. Society of Jesus.

SL   Strachan Letterbooks.

SP   Strachan Papers.

SPG   Missionary Reports and Letters from Canada. Society for the Propagation of the Gospel in Foreign Parts.

Government Documents

AT 1834   Aboriginal Tribes. 1834. Great Britain, Colonial Office.

BNA
Provinces   British North American Provinces. 1839. Great Britain, Colonial Office.

CR 1847   Report on the Affairs of the Indians in Canada, laid before the Legislative Assembly, 1845-1846. Canada, Indian Department.

CR 1858   Report, 1858. Canada, Indian Department.

BIBLIOGRAPHY

Manuscripts

Archives of the Church Missionary Society. London. Wilson Letters.

Archives of the Society for the Propagation of the Gospel in Foreign Parts. London. Missionary Reports and Letters.

Archives of the United Church, Victoria College. Toronto. Methodist Missionary Notices (microfilm).

Department of Public Records and Archives of Ontario. Toronto. Strachan Letterbooks. Strachan Papers.

Public Archives of Canada. Ottawa. Record Group 10, Indian Affairs Papers.

Regis College Library. Toronto. Jennesseaux and Du Ranquet Letters (copies).

Toronto Public Library. William Jarvis Papers.

Published Government Reports

Canada, Indian Department.
    1846-47. Report on the Affairs of the Indians in Canada, laid before the Legislative Assembly, 1845-1846. 2 vols, Montreal.

    1858. Special commissioners appointed on the 8th of September, 1856, to Investigate Indian affairs in Canada. Report. Toronto.

Great Britain, Colonial Office.
    1834. Aboriginal Tribes (North America, New South Wales, Van Dieman's Land, and British Guiana). Parliamentary Paper No. 617.

    1839. British North American Provinces, Return to an Address of the Honourable the House of Commons Dated 11 June 1839, for Copies of Extracts of Correspondence since 1st April 1835 Between the Secretary of State for the Colonies and the Governors of the British North American Provinces Respecting the Indians in those Provinces. Parliamentary Paper No. 323.

Published Missionary Reports

Baptist Missionary Convention of the State of New York. *Annual Reports.*

The British North American Wesleyan Methodist Magazine.

Canada Baptist Union. *Annual Reports.*

Canadian Ecclesiastical Gazette.

The Canadian Independent.

Christian Advocate and Journal.

Christian Guardian.

Church Missionary Society. *Proceedings.*

Corporation for the Promoting and Propagating of the Gospel of Jesus Christ in New England, London. *Reports; History, 1871; Six Years Summary, 1879.*

Methodist Episcopal Church Missionary Society in Canada. *Annual Reports.*

Methodist Magazine (New York).

Missionary Society of the Wesleyan Methodist Church in Canada, in connexion with the English Conference. *Annual Reports.*

Society for Converting and Civilizing the Indians and Propagating the Gospel among Destitute Settlers in Upper Canada. *Reports.*

Society for the Propagation of the Gospel in Foreign Parts. *Reports. The Church in the Colonies. Proceedings.*

The United Brethren. Missionary Intelligencer and Religious Miscellany. *Periodical Accounts. Proceedings of the Society for the Propagation of the Gospel among the Heathen.*

Wesleyan Missionary Notices.

Books and Articles

Banton, Michael. 1965. *Roles.* London: Tavistock Publications.

Beaven, James. 1846. *Recreations of a Long Vacation: or, A visit to Indian Missions in Upper Canada.* London.

Berkhofer, Robert F. Jr. 1965. *Salvation and the Savage.* University of Kentucky Press.

———. 1965. Faith and Factionalism among the Senecas: Theory and Ethnohistory. *Ethnohistory* 12:99-112.

Bliss, Eugene F., ed. and trans. 1885. *Diary of David Zeisberger.* Cincinnati.

Clark, A.J., ed. 1932. Earliest Missionary Letters of the Rev. John Douse, from the Salt Springs Mission on the Grand River in 1834 and 1836. Ontario Historical Society, *Papers and Records* 28:41-6.

Copway, George. 1847 (1851). *The Life History and Travels of Kay-ge-ga-gah-Bowh (George Copway)*. Albany: printed by Weed and Parsons.

Findlay, G.G. and Holdsworth, W.W. 1921-4. *The History of the Wesleyan Methodist Missionary Society*. London: Epworth Press.

Graham, Elizabeth. 1968. Christianity and the Khoi Khoin: A Study of the Roles of Missionaries as Contact Agents. Unpublished Phil.M. thesis, University of Toronto.

——. 1973. Strategies and Souls. Unpublished PhD Thesis, University of Toronto.

Gray, Elma and L.R. 1956. *Wilderness Christians: The Moravian Mission to the Delaware Indians*. Toronto: The Macmillan Company of Canada Ltd.

Indian Chiefs and Principal Men. General Council, Orillia. 1846. *Minutes . . . of the General Council. . . . On the proposed removal of the smaller communities and the establishment of Manual Labour Schools. . . . Montreal*.

Jacobs, Peter. 1858. *Journal of the Rev. Peter Jacobs*. New York.

Jacobson, Henry A. 1895. Narrative of an Attempt to Establish a Mission among the Chippewa Indians of Canada. Moravian Historical Society, *Transactions* 5:part 1.

Jenness, Diamond. 1955. *The Indians of Canada*. Ottawa: National Museum of Canada.

Johnston, C.M., ed. 1964. *The Valley of the Six Nations*. The Champlain Society for the Government of Ontario: University of Toronto Press.

Jones, Peter. 1860. *Life and Journals of Kah-ke-wa-quo-na-by (Rev. Peter Jones), Wesleyan Missionary*. Toronto: Anson Green.

——. 1861. *History of the Ojebway Indians*. London.

Landon, Fred. 1930. Selections from the papers of James Evans, Missionary to the Indians. Ontario Historical Society, *Papers and Records* 26:474-491.

Lydekker, John W. 1938. *The Faithful Mohawks*. Cambridge University Press.

Morris, J.L. 1943. *Indians of Ontario.* Toronto: Ontario Government Department of Lands and Forests.

Nadel, S.F. 1957. *The Theory of Social Structure.* London: Cohen and West.

Newcomb, W. 1956. *The Culture and Acculturation of the Delaware Indians.* Ann Arbor: University of Michigan.

Pascoe, C.F. 1901. *Two hundred years of the S.P.G.: an historical account of the Society for the propagation of the gospel in foreign parts, 1701-1900.* London: published at the Society's Office.

Pryse, J.P. 1963-4. Pioneer Baptist Missionaries to Upper Canada Tuscaroras. *Canadian Baptist Home Missions Digest* 6:273-282.

———. 1969. The Rev. James N. Cusick 1805-61. *Link and Visitor* 42:21.

Pyne, A. 1875. *Reminiscences of Colonial Life and Missionary Adventure in both Hemispheres.* London.

Radcliffe, The Rev. T., ed. 1953 *Authentic Letters from Upper Canada; with an account of Canadian Field Sports.* By T.W. Magrath Esq. Toronto: The Macmillan Company of Canada Ltd. (First published 1833, Dublin: William Curry, Jr. and Company).

Radin, Paul. 1914. *Some Myths and Tales of the Ojibwa of Southeastern Ontario.* Canada Dept. of Mines, Geological Survey, Memoir 48, No. 2, Anthropological series. Ottawa.

———. 1914. An Introductory Enquiry in the Study of Ojibwa Religion. Ontario Historical Society, *Papers and Records* 12:210-218.

Torry, The Rev. Alvin. 1864. *Autobiography of Rev. Alvin Torry.* Auburn: William J. Moses.

Van Dusen, Conrad. 1867. *The Indian Chief.* London: printed by W. Nichols.

Waddilove, William J.D., ed. 1838. *The Stewart Missions.* London: J. Hatchard and Son.

Wallman, Sandra. 1974. Status and the Innovator. In *Choice and Change,* ed. John Davis. LSE Monograph on Social Anthropology no. 50. London: Athlone Press.

West, John. 1827. *A Journal of a Mission to the Indians of the British Provinces of New Brunswick and Nova Scotia, and the Mohawks on the Ouse or Grand River, Upper Canada.* London.

Wilson, Edward F. 1856. *Missionary Work among the Ojibway Indians.* S.P.C.K.

Young, A.H., ed. 1922. The Rev. Robert Addison: Extracts from the Reports and (Manuscript) Journals of Society for the Propagation of the Gospel in Foreign Parts. Ontario Historical Society, *Papers and Records* 19:171-191.

INDEX